Drummond

Life

THE DISCRIMINATING THIEF

THE DISCRIMINATING THIEF

Xavier Richier and The Château Gang

by

DAVID LEITCH

HODDER AND STOUGHTON

SBN 340 02556 5

*Printed in Great Britain for Hodder and Stoughton Limited, St. Paul's House,
Warwick Lane, London, E.C.4 by Northumberland Press Limited, Gateshead*

ACKNOWLEDGEMENTS

This book had its genesis in April, 1965 with an "Insight" article on the Château Gang in *The Sunday Times* of London. The gestation period has been longer than anyone, including myself, ever expected. It would never have begun without my *Sunday Times* colleagues, Bruce Page and Colin Simpson, who originally intended to collaborate with me on the book, but were eventually forced to drop out through pressure of other work. Many of the people who helped me so generously in France will have to remain unacknowledged because of the law of "professional secrecy" which is designed to prevent delicate information reaching third parties, particularly when they are reporters. However I can thank many of the Gang's victims who assisted me, notably Madame Geneviève Fath; the Duc de Luynes; the Comte Robert de Dampierre; and Mr. George Stacey. In Paris Mlle. Danielle Dumon and Comte Odon de Quinsonas gave much of their time, as did M. Jean-Pierre Hagnauer. M. Jacques Dupont of the Historic Monuments department was generous with both time and expertise.

The ninth chapter "How They Destroyed Versailles" owes its information on the fluctuations of French furniture prices in the nineteenth century and since, to the acknowledged authority in the field, Mr. Gerald Reitlinger, whose book, *The Economics of Taste, Part Two: Objets d'Art, 1760-1960*, tells the whole story, and much more. In London Miss Sally Turner and Miss Margaret Laing read proofs and made valuable suggestions. Mrs. Jenni Davies, who later performed the same unenviable task with *Philby*, indefatigably typed the manuscript and its various revisions. My agent, Miss Diana Crawfurd, was an unfailing source of encouragement and perceptive advice. A distinguished French judge recently expressed his surprise that valuable antiques owned privately are virtually uninsurable; annual premiums usually run at between one quarter and

5

ACKNOWLEDGEMENTS

one third of the total value, and the same prohibitive system applies in many other countries. This book is not intended to be censorious—it was often written to make a break from grimmer topics. But insofar as it contains a moral it is for amateur collectors who, guarding against reincarnations of Xavier Richier, might well apply the Prophet Job's terse advice on the subject of daughters to their own antiques. Lock them up.

CONTENTS

ILLUSTRATIONS

(following page 12)

[1] Ziolo.
[2] United Press International.
[3] *Sunday Times.*

9

CHAPTER I

How They Robbed the Duc de Luynes

It was an insolent operation, even by the high standards of a gang who had already proved that they were probably the most skilful antique thieves who have ever existed. Like so many of their thefts, it was carried out with almost absurd ease. It was an undramatic, pastoral scene—a French country house at dusk. The three main actors, one cast unknowingly in the role of dupe, met in front of the elegant Château de Dampierre. All three were strolling along the well kept path that winds round the west wing of the house; it was just after six in the evening of May 23rd, 1963. An idyllic, somnolent evening.

Jean Charbonneau, *régisseur* or bailiff of the Château de Dampierre, had a clear conscience, unlike the other two men. He was also by far the most agitated. He was angry to see two strangers still on the premises at that time; it was very irritating because he wanted to complete locking up and get back to his quarters in the west wing. There was a variety programme on television that he was particularly anxious not to miss. He descended on the two men and asked them what they thought they were doing in the grounds.

One of them was small and slight, with exceptionally long brown hair flopping over his ears, an aquiline nose, and gentle, evasive eyes. He said nothing. But his companion, a strong, solid man, carrying a canvas sack, and wearing a neat, metropolitan

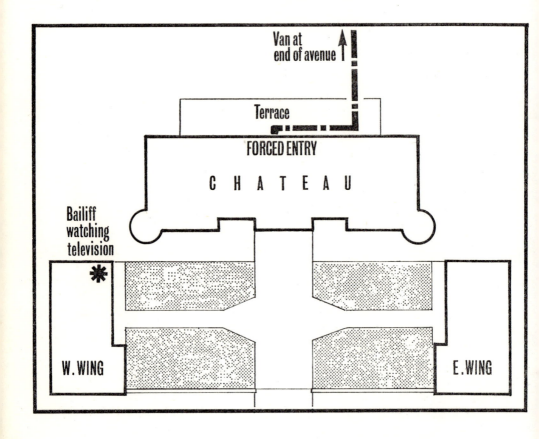

How Mabilotte and Huré broke into Dampierre

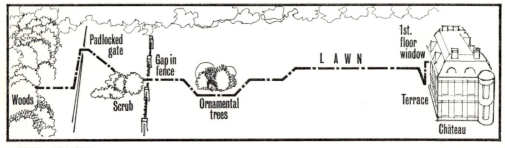

PETER SULLEVAN

The Duke de Luynes' Château of Dampierre, raided by the syndicate in May, 1963

The Count of Bussy-Rabutin, rake, soldier of fortune, duellist and collector

Bussy's "Gallery of Virgins"

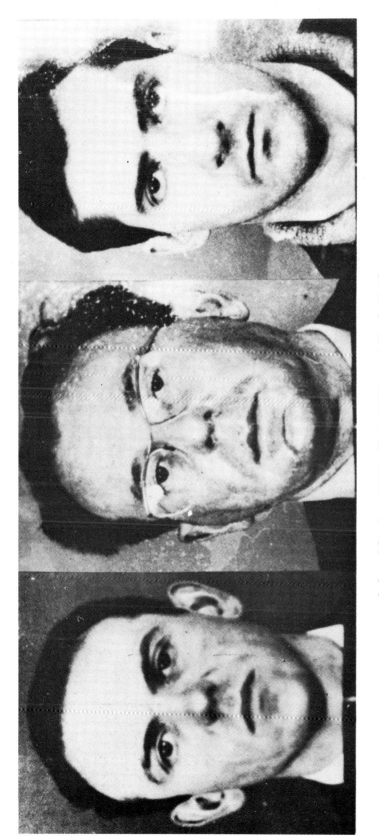

Left to right: Jean Richier, Xavier Richier and Claude Mabilotte

Xavier Richier's bijou museum at Liévin

A Louis XVI *fauteuil*, stolen by the syndicate and recovered to Marcel Bihn's specification

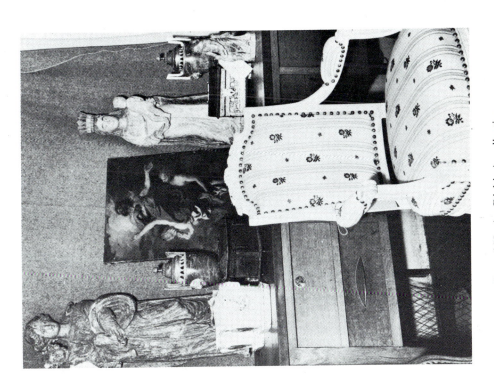

Part of Xavier Richier's collection

Another view of Dampierre. The thieves entered by the left hand of the three first floor windows under the pediment and left by the centre door on the floor below.

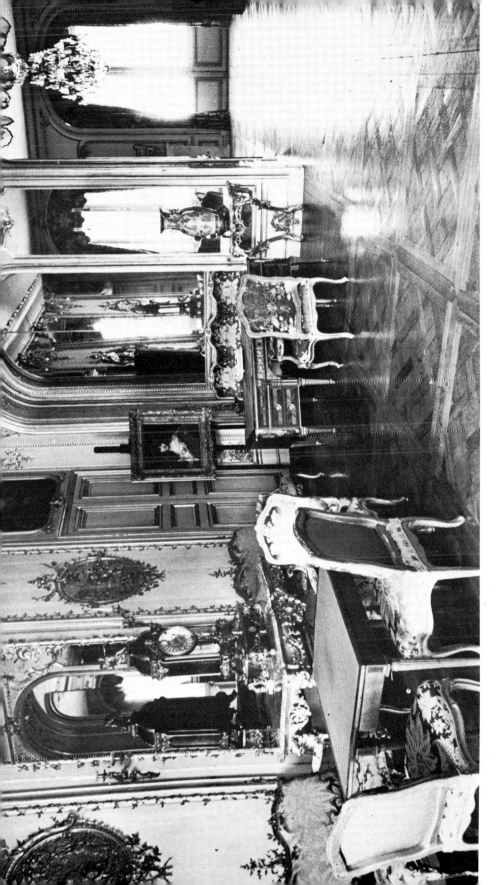

The *grand salon* at Dampierre

One of the tapestries of the Holy Martyrs stolen from Le Mans Cathedral

The altar of St. Denis and the solid silver altar-piece which was
removed from it

The Bouboulis china cabinet before the theft. Only the plates visible on top two and bottom shelves were removed—they alone bore the rare double arrow mark

Château of Bussy-le-Grand from which the syndicate removed four signed Boulard chairs, ignoring sixteen virtually indistinguishable contemporary copies

Part of Alain Michel's
magpie collection

The Chandelier of
St. Peter's Cathedral in
Poitiers after Michel
had "converted" it

suit, answered Charbonneau's question at once. He said he was
a restorer, visiting the château with his assistant. "We've come to
collect the *secrétaire*—the Duc de Luynes gave us the instructions."

Charbonneau had heard nothing about these restorations before but he accepted the explanation without question. Tourists,
photographers, friends of the Duke, God knows who else—they
were always turning up without appointments, and no one ever
bothered to tell *him*. For a while he complained about the difficulties of being a bailiff. Neither of the two men spoke. Finally
Charbonneau told them there was nothing they could do except
return in two days, when the Duke was expected at the house.
"There's no one here now"—and he shrugged with that gesture
familiar to anyone who has ever unsuccessfully solicited information in France. The two men accepted the situation
equably enough, the big man throwing his bag over his shoulder
as they walked off. Charbonneau assumed it contained something to do with restoring, a subject about which he had only
the vaguest idea. He did not even bother to see them out of
the massive main gates, which he was shortly going to lock for
the night. Unfortunately for the Duke, neither the men nor
their bag interested his bailiff half as much as his television programme.

Because it is within such convenient range of Paris—thirty
miles along the autoroute, and not more than fifty minutes' drive
from the centre except during the morning and evening rush
hours—the Château de Dampierre, one of France's most important country houses, receives visitors all the time. Unchanged
since the architect, Jules Hardouin-Mansart, rebuilt it towards
the end of the seventeenth century for the ancestors of the present Duc de Luynes, who still owns the domain, the house understandably figures prominently in all the guide books. In the
eighteenth century Dampierre often served as the residence of
Marie Leczinska, wife of Louis XV, as the Duchesse de Luynes
of the period was her chief lady-in-waiting. The cost of providing endless exotic dinners for the Queen was said to have reduced the Duc, an exceptionally mean and dull man, to a
state of acute depression. Later on, under the second empire,

the Duc Honoré commissioned Ingres to paint a series of frescos in the *grande salle*; the great painter agreed graciously on condition that no one should be allowed to enter until his work was completed. One day the Duc Honoré sneaked in when Ingres was away—many months had elapsed since the commission. To his fury the Duc found that only one fresco was completed; another had been started, but only very sketchily. Ingres had been using the *grande salle* of Dampierre as a luxurious studio; it was crammed with other pieces that he and his students had been working on. The Duc threw them all out, so Dampierre now has one and a half Ingres frescos, another item among its eclectic range of fine furniture and pictures gathered over two and a half centuries. It is one of the most brilliantly furnished houses in France. Although surrounded by a moat it is not fortified in any sense; it is built on the usual seventeenth-century H-shaped plan, the cross bar of the H being the main section of the house which contains the grand salon on the ground floor. The Duc and his family normally live in Paris but from time to time they pass a few days in a section of the west wing. Apart from Jean Charbonneau's quarters, the rest of the house is uninhabited. The bailiff is an easy-going, not particularly terrifying figure, but his presence alone had been quite enough to frighten André Huré, the smaller of the two "restorers", very badly. His reflex was to go straight back to Paris. Claude Mabilotte, his brawny and more confident companion, was made of sterner stuff. He insisted that the bailiff would never be able to identify them again. In any case he had been attracted by the château because it offered him an easy way of earning 14,000 new francs (£1,000) and he was determined not to give up until he had earned his money. The two men argued for some time just outside the main gates, now firmly locked, but there was no doubt who was going to win. Claude Mabilotte suggested they settle the matter over dinner in the village. Reinforced by a bottle of beaujolais and Claude Mabilotte's arguments, Huré finally agreed to go ahead with the operation, despite this minor mishap.

By eight-thirty the two thieves had hidden Huré's Deux-Chevaux estate wagon with its Paris plates, 7541 JM 75, off the road to Chevreuse. They approached the château by the back entrance, making their way cautiously down the wooded hillside, until they reached the fence at the bottom, the château's outer defence. From here they walked fifty yards east until they came to a gate with an ancient padlock. Before they reached it, Mabilotte had already taken a twelve inch metal bar from his canvas bag; he cracked the lock with the expertise of someone who had done the same thing many times before. From here the two men branched half right through the gate and headed for a patch of scrub. It stood only yards from the château's second defence, a metal fence with vertical bars, but four of them were missing— wide enough to drive a small car through. Without any hesitation whatever, the men had arrived at the weak spot. They knew exactly what they were looking for—the terrain had been examined and prepared in advance. Ahead some ornamental trees, then a stretch of roughly 200 yards of dead flat, open ground leading directly to the château, its shape looming heavily in the darkness like an ocean liner. Most of the ground here was raked earth—they neatly skirted it, keeping to a convenient stretch of lawn. Finally they arrived on the terrace in front of the tall glass doors which lead to the grand salon. As they knew in advance, these were locked and bolted—from the inside. They did not even consider breaking them; it would have been too noisy and, apart from that, unaesthetic. These burglars were far too sophisticated for anything so crude.

Instead, Mabilotte opened his sack again and produced a length of hooked rope. He knew, from previous reconnaissances, that the shutters on the first floor would be open. He attached his rope to a series of convenient protuberances in the stonework, and shinned up with an agility unlikely in so bulky a man. He set to work with a brace and bit on the window frame to the left of the main column, drilling a hole thirty millimetres in diameter. He took a screwdriver out of his bag and poked it through. All he had to do was lift the latch and let himself through the open window.

The next day Inspector Louis Raton, a French policeman who had spent the previous three years trying to get his hands on the gang that had been systematically pillaging French country houses, received an emergency call from Dampierre.

Raton, a cheerful, philosophic figure who fortunately had long acquired the habit of taking life as it comes, began by checking the method of entry. When he saw the hole in the window frame he produced a massive Gallic shrug. It told him everything; he had seen many virtually identical window frames in the past, even the hole was always the same diameter. Without examining an inventory of the contents Raton already had a pretty exact idea of what kind of furniture had been stolen; it was sure to be of the eighteenth century, doubtless the finest examples that the Duke owned. Claude Mabilotte's personal style could not have been more distinctive if he had scratched his signature on the window pane. After three years the police had come to recognise it; they were still no nearer finding out who this particularly expert burglar was.

It had taken Mabilotte just under ten minutes to get into the château. Once through the window he walked across the main gallery, crossed the upper salon cautiously, masking his torch. He had already been warned that his weight would cause the big chandeliers in the grand salon downstairs to vibrate with a fairly loud tinkling noise, so when he heard the sounds he was not worried. He knew that the *régisseur* was in his room 150 yards away in the west wing; by now he had probably gone to bed. Mabilotte opened the grand salon doors and Huré, waiting on the terrace, came in. As burglaries go it was neat, economical and well planned, but otherwise unremarkable. Any one of several hundred professionals in Paris could have performed an equally competent job. But now the two men demonstrated the particular technique which set the château gang apart, and had accounted for their remarkable success. They walked directly to the right hand side of the salon where four of the twelve chairs in the room were set round a small dining table. They carried these to the large doors, ready to be shifted out via the terrace, and completely ignored the crowded contents of the rest of the room—perhaps a hundred and fifty separate objects in all, including a Louis XV commode of extraordinary quality, one of the finest extant, which would probably fetch £20,000 at an open sale at Sotheby's or Christie's. They ignored this magnificent object because it had not been ordered; Huré

16

and Mabilotte were only interested in items on a list they had already learnt by heart. These were, apart from the chairs, three women's writing desks, technically known as *bonheurs du jour*, which they brought down one at a time, carrying each between them, from the rear gallery on the first floor. From the same floor they took one *Régence* bureau; a Louis XV *écritoire*; and a pair of mid-eighteenth-century vases, delicate copies in faïence of Roman amphorae. This was the total haul. They did not even bother to look at the many portable and valuable objects —silver cigarette cases, gold gilt clocks—that covered every available surface. They were not in the least interested in this record of the Luynes family's aristocratic whims and acquisitive urges over the previous two hundred years. By the time Mabilotte brought the last objects on the list, the amphorae, down from the first floor it was ten o'clock and they were both sweating.

Again they worked in stages. First all the furniture was moved on to the terrace, then to the inner fence 200 yards away. When they were ready to move the last pair of tables Mabilotte punctiliously closed the large doors behind them. They had been kept open until then because they offered one possible escape route (through the house) if anyone had arrived while they were working. The transfer of the furniture was the most vulnerable stage of the operation; it had lasted just thirty minutes. Once they had moved all the objects as far as the first fence the whole thing was as good as over.

In a series of journeys, backwards and forwards, they advanced to the second fence. Then the long and most exhausting phase of all, moving the pieces one at a time through the wood to the Deux-Chevaux. As they had calculated, they were able to fit exactly half the items inside. They accordingly transported these to a pre-arranged patch of scrub bushes one mile west along the Chevreuse road. They hid them here in the bushes, returned, loaded their wagon with the remainder, and with Huré driving arrived in Paris seventy-five minutes later. The little man drove with elaborate caution and was extremely punctilious about stop signs and traffic lights, in contrast to the cavalier style of driving which he adopted when the van was "clean". At one a.m. they arrived at their destination; a large, by now deserted block of flats in the Place Léon-Blum, just off the Boulevard Voltaire. A slight young man in jeans was waiting for them, and between them they carried the contents up the red-carpeted staircase to the first floor and flat No. 6, marked with a brass decorative bell, and a coconut mat with the initials "J.R." As soon as all the items were inside, taking their place alongside an already impressive collection of mainly eighteenth-century antiques, Huré descended to the van and, driving faster now, headed back the way they had come. He was going to collect the rest of the furniture they had left behind.

While they waited for him Mabilotte and the young man in jeans, whose name was Jean Richier, drank and talked. There was no one to overhear them for though Jean Richier lived with his mother he had put her to bed hours earlier with the warm milk and sleeping pill she was accustomed to take every night. Mabilotte, who did not share Jean's tender feelings either for his mother, or for the Boulard chairs from Dampierre which the young man was now examining, was thinking only of the money he would get for the job. Jean stroked the carved back of a *fauteuil*, feeling the delicate tendrils of wood to which the eighteenth-century carver would have devoted days or even weeks, knowing that time and expense were of no importance. The only criterion had been perfection. Mabilotte lolled back, letting his nerves settle, and making no attempt to conceal his contempt for Jean's aesthetic raptures. Now the young man had upended one of the chairs to confirm that the *estampille* of Boulard, the mastermaker's personal signature, was stamped into the frame. Mabilotte was only interested in such details insofar as they increased the value of the furniture; to him one old chair looked very like another. For this reason he needed expert guidance, which he received from Jean Richier and even more from Jean's elder brother, Xavier. If Mabilotte had broken into Dampierre without their detailed briefing, and tried to work in the dark, he would probably only have succeeded in stealing a load of heavy and virtually worthless Victorian furniture. It was so difficult not to be deceived by imitations, no matter how one studied the eighteenth-century furniture makers, and at one stage Mabilotte had gone so far as to do some homework for himself in the hope of acquiring enough expertise to be able to work independently. But no longer; Mabilotte was no aesthete but he had plenty of common sense. He had never particularly liked the Richier brothers—their affectations and air of superiority irritated him—but he realised they were necessary to him. For over two years now they had provided him with a higher—and steadier—income than he had ever imagined possible, except for occasional dreams of winning the national lottery. Satisfied that the furniture was exactly what he had ordered, Jean Richier decided that he must get in touch with his brother at once. Xavier lived outside Paris in a small town called Liévin, 120 miles north-east. He invariably made a point of having nothing to do with the break-in operations, preferring to give his orders from a safe distance. This was a great relief to Mabilotte, who found Xavier Richier one of the most infuriating men he had ever come across. Jean was still chattering excitedly to his elder brother on the telephone when Huré returned with the rest of the Dampierre loot. In ten minutes they had set it out with the first batch in Jean's apartment. In the course of one evening they had succeeded in stealing furniture to the value of roughly £50,000. Now all they had to do was to sell it.

CHAPTER II

The Syndicate Forms

Exactly a fortnight later the four Paris partners in the art theft syndicate met in a cramped workshop, its floor littered with wood shavings. They were at 5, rue de Charonne, the street where most of the furniture restoring—and faking—in Paris is carried out. Jean Richier, Claude Mabilotte and André Huré were all feeling exceptionally confident and pleased with themselves. But this did not stop them deferring to the fourth colleague. As usual Marcel Bihn, who was a natural leader, assumed the centre of the stage. Marcel's regular features were set off by a deep tan; a shade under six feet two inches, he was wearing a dark suit which had been recently pressed. Only a slight exaggeration in the roll of the lapels gave away the fact that it was a Faubourg St. Honoré imitation of Savile Row, not the real thing.

If Marcel had been a professional con man, which he might easily have been had things turned out slightly differently, he would have found no difficulty in masquerading as a successful merchant banker with sporting instincts, or an upper class army officer on leave. The last thing he looked like was an antiques thief, which was one of the reasons why the syndicate found him so valuable. His speciality was disguising stolen furniture, and disposing of it.

Marcel had called at Jean's flat the morning after the Dampierre theft. One look at the Duc de Luynes' chairs and he had decided that the most effective (and cheapest) method of disguise was to remove the gilt to reveal the original unvarnished wood. Jean and André had started to strip the chairs at once. Now, two weeks later, anyone who had known the chairs in their previous existence, set round the dining table in the grand salon at Dampierre, would have found it hard to recognise them. But the centre chair of the set presented more of a problem. Its lines were sinuous and elegant, like everything Boulard produced, but as the centrepiece it had been designed with massive arms and a heavy back-rest elaborately carved with flowers. A fairly complicated conversion was necessary to ensure that no one would ever be able to recognise it, and Marcel had spent a long time discussing the matter with Christopher Gonzalez-Sotto, the restorer who owned the workshop. Then he had decided what was required. Gonzalez-Sotto would recarve the chair's arms, obliterating all the floral decoration; he would carry out a similar operation on the back-rest but preserve one piece of the original carving, a large rose in the centre. The craftsman calculated it could be done in a week. Over the years he and his colleague in the workshop above, a *tapissier* or specialist upholsterer called Robert Massé, had carried out a great deal of work of this kind, much of it legitimate, some more doubtful. They made it a point never to ask questions.

Massé was briefed next. Marcel explained that the chairs were to be recovered with a faded length of authentic eighteenth-century tapestry which Jean had acquired, from where only he knew. All the syndicate realised that when Bihn's instructions had been carried out the value of the chairs would be considerably reduced. Changing the seat covers was comparatively unimportant; removing the original, finely preserved gilding was barbaric; botching and obliterating the carving was almost sacrilegious.

Xavier Richier, who fortunately for his Paris colleagues was safely out of the way, would undoubtedly have made an issue of the matter. The doctor was fond of money and totally dishonest but he felt genuinely, even fanatically, about eighteenth-century furniture, and operations of this kind were anathema to him. His colleagues regarded him as an affected *poseur*.

They knew that the chair's appearance would be ruined and

its real value halved but aesthetic considerations were, for them, irrelevant. Marcel was a businessman, not a connoisseur, and the Paris end of the syndicate agreed wholeheartedly with his approach. This was especially true of Claude Mabilotte, who had always fancied himself as a business executive, liked to use the business jargon he had picked up from a correspondence course in marketing he had once begun (and never finished), and, in contrast to the camp outfits which appealed to Jean and André, always dressed in sober grey. Claude's actual business experience, despite his aspirations, had been limited, largely because the concept of a regular job had never appealed to him. Like André, his partner in most of the château raids, and Jean Richier, he had spent most of his adult life supporting himself erratically on the fringe of the legitimate Paris antiques trade.

They all called themselves "decorators" (of the three Jean's claim to the title was the most genuine) but in fact they all belonged to a rather small, quintessentially Parisian sub-sector of the French antiques business. They worked as *brocanteurs* or *chineurs*, both slang words without a precise English equivalent. *Brocanteurs* are small dealers without the capital, or knowledge, to handle important pieces, but with a certain limited flair which enables them to make a modest living buying and selling items of no great value. The three had originally met when they were all working on stalls at St. Ouen, the Flea Market on the northern outskirts of Paris, selling eclectic bric-à-brac, often to tourists. Jean and André both had a good eye for the ephemeral fashions of Camp decoration; Claude was an accomplished salesman. Later they had graduated to working as assistants in small shops in the area of the rue de Seine on the Left Bank, one stage up from the Flea Market but still a long way removed from the important dealers. Jean had by now acquired a certain reputation as a *chineur*—a middleman with a gift for smelling out an interesting object, often at an auction sale, which he would then resell to a dealer. By the late 'fifties Jean was sufficiently well known to work on margin. He had an expert knowledge of the specialities of several scores of small shops on the Left Bank for whom he operated as a middleman. He would see something, telephone a dealer, and describe it. Invariably the dealer would give him permission to buy it in his own name, sometimes with one of his own cheques, and guarantee him a commission of between ten and twenty per cent (the dealer himself would always resell with a "mark-up" of seventy-five per cent, and sometimes much more). It was an easy way of earning a living, but not a very lucrative one. Jean scoured Paris incessantly, travelling by Metro, and had never managed to average more than £30 a week, or at least until he had started to exploit his knowledge of antiques in a very different and far less legitimate direction.

Jean and André were both homosexual; Claude was a dedicated womaniser, married at twenty and separated three years later. All three had acquired the mannerisms of a style common to London and New York as well as Paris—Decorators' Camp. They haunted sales looking for likely objects, succeeded occasionally in pulling off a commission to decorate a small shop or a bistro, made friends where they could, and never aspired to the kind of scholarship that makes a fine-art expert. They were happy enough if they could pick out a piece of apparent junk that, given a coat of paint or a new pair of legs, might be turned into an "amusing" object that someone would pay £25 for. But they knew that there was little chance that any of them would ever manage to make a serious career as either dealers or decorators. To begin with they would never have enough capital to set themselves up.

They had got into the habit of working together; all three cast round for an opening, a break-through, anything that would enable them to develop, and not spend the next ten years in the same marginal way. Claude was the most impatient and in 1956 he had cut one corner too many; he was jailed for a year after being arrested for a series of petty frauds. André had kept out of trouble with the police. He lacked Claude's bravado, and also his ever-pressing economic motivations. André had a talent for finding middle-aged men who were prepared, even willing, to subsidise him. Jean was an immature, boyish figure, and for several years he was perfectly content with his modest existence. Eventually he changed; his mother and brother had always cherished ambitions of a grander life and Jean finally came round to sharing them. He realised that he could not spend the rest of his life as an ageing student.

They were all psychologically ready to try something new, in Claude's case virtually anything new, and when in 1959 Dr. Xavier Richier began to sound them out they were all gratifyingly impressed by his nervous eloquence. They had all known for a long time that most French country houses have inadequate, and sometimes non-existent security protection against intruders, but they had never thought about exploiting this omission. Xavier persuaded them that country house thefts would be easy (he also said it was their duty as civilised men to remove and restore objects which were being allowed to decay, an argument they treated with greater scepticism). At the end of 1959 and the beginning of 1960 they had begun to steal, cautiously testing themselves and developing their expertise. It had been as easy as Xavier had said. By 1962 they were confident that they had discovered an easy way of getting rich, one the police were too ignorant to find out about, or stop.

They extended their operations and raided some of the most famous houses in the country. By the end of 1962 France was in the grip of a wave of major art thefts.

The thefts themselves were the easiest part of the operation. Xavier chose the houses, assessed the furniture, made a list of objects to be removed, and Claude and André set off in their van. Nothing to it. With churches and cathedrals it was even simpler. But it was one thing to acquire rare objects and quite another to sell them. Xavier insisted on keeping some of the best things for his own collection and Jean, whose job it was to organise the disposal of the remainder, had failed to find a systematic and safe method. They sold furniture haphazardly, often for a fraction of its real value. But then the thieves had a stroke of luck.

The Piscine Deligny, a large open-air swimming pool on the Left Bank, was one of André Huré's favourite places on summer afternoons. On a boiling June day in 1961 he was sitting by the water in his miniscule bikini when he noticed a huge, athletic man with a fine intellectual head standing on the diving platform. Unlike André himself, who was deeply tanned, the big man's skin had a wintry pallor.

Curious, and interested, André went over and opened a conversation. He discovered the man's name was Marcel Bihn and that he had spent most of the previous three years working for the *Algerie-Française* movement. Marcel had allowed his passion for a French Algeria to get him on the wrong side of the police, who suspected that he had worked for the Secret Army Organisation, the O.A.S., which had initiated a series of terrorist outrages, and also assassination attempts against General de Gaulle. Marcel had just been released from prison after a spell of internment as a political detainee, and he was looking for something to do.

André had started the conversation with vague thoughts of seduction but as he listened to the big man he began to wonder about bringing him into the syndicate. Marcel, it appeared, had relations in Algeria, and after serving there as an officer had spent most of his time working for various extreme right-wing political groups. Marcel was tough and unscrupulous but also fanatically devoted to keeping Algeria French. The O.A.S. was imbued with an empire-building ideology; it had provided a haven for unstable idealists as well as neo-fascists, gangsters, and petty crooks on the make. Marcel, like so many other disaffiliated army officers, had been attracted to the O.A.S. on several different levels. But no more. He was now working part-time for a perfectly respectable organisation helping French nationals who had been repatriated from Algeria, and avoiding his political friends. One taste of prison had been enough. Unlike many of his former comrades Marcel was hardheaded enough to see that *Algérie-Française* was dead; he had no taste for martyrdom.

André was a good listener and he had a quick, clever gift for getting people to talk and assessing them. He encouraged Marcel to continue, and told him that a close friend of his (a certain "Bruno" Bunau-Varilla who was to play a minor but interesting role in the later history of the château syndicate) had also been a political detainee. In the course of several afternoons at the pool André extracted a good deal of biographical information from Marcel, and reached an important decision. He discovered that Marcel's mother was called Bella-Gamba (a name Marcel sometimes used himself) and that for many years she had owned a high-class antiques shop on the Quai Voltaire, not far from the Piscine Deligny, where she specialised in fine lithographs. She had a good reputation in the Paris antiques trade and though he was not an expert Marcel knew his way about. Before his military service he had graduated at the École du Louvre, a more exclusive and academic version of the "Arts-Déco" where Jean Richier had studied (with little distinction). Marcel, it turned out, was a collector in a modest way, and something of an expert on restoration (it had been his special subject at the school). André decided that his new friend had knowledge, contacts, style, organising ability, and a total lack of scruple. He was also short of money. Marcel Bihn was exactly what the syndicate needed.

André went about the delicate business of "selling" Marcel to the syndicate—and the syndicate to Marcel—with Byzantine subtlety, telling everyone a slightly different story, and convincing them all that it was in their own personal interest to bring in this fiery intellectual tough. Claude agreed enthusiastically; he was sold on Marcel as a hard-headed pragmatist, who had learnt something about administration in the army, and would organise the syndicate's activities with a minimum of aesthetic posturing. Jean was taken with Marcel personally and was impressed by his contacts—through his mother Marcel knew most of the important functionaries at the Hotel Drouot, the leading sale-room. He also had friends who were collectors and well-established, legitimate dealers. Jean was relieved at the prospect of having someone else responsible for most of the furniture; he found the job a strain. To André's surprise, Xavier also accepted the idea equably enough; as long as he decided what objects were to be stolen, and could be sure of keeping anything that especially appealed to him for his collection, he affected not to be concerned at the commercial operation in Paris. (André suspected that Xavier liked the idea of them making more money, as long as he was not overtly involved himself.) Marcel did not hesitate and he immediately suggested a way of developing the syndicate—they should buy a shop of their own. Late in 1962 he found cheap, central premises and with André as his partner opened a shop in the Quai Malaquais on the Left Bank overlooking the river.

Marcel soon proved his skill at judging how individual pieces could be restored or modified, either as a disguise, or in some cases to improve its immediate commercial appeal. The Dampierre *fauteuils*, after he had supervised their alterations, were sold by Marcel personally. Here he used a personal contact, an honest dealer called Graziani, who was an old friend of his mother, Madame Bella-Gamba, with a shop near hers on the Quai Voltaire.

Graziani had known Marcel since he was a child and accepted his story about where the chairs had come from without questioning its veracity. He was able to resell them, in perfectly good faith and at a satisfactory profit, to an impeccably respectable dealer called Weiler. The syndicate had acquired two valuable, legitimate outlets, both above suspicion, and made nearly £10,000, much more than they had expected.

They used the Quai Malaquais shop as a front and found from the end of 1962 onwards, that it was now comparatively simple to funnel "hot", though often disguised furniture into the legitimate trade. Jean was free to do what he liked best. The word had got around that he had a flair for producing remarkably distinguished furniture at modest prices; for the first time he found himself in demand as a serious decorator. Jean would recommend specific pieces for a client's apartment, check with Xavier where they could be stolen, arrange for Claude and André to carry out the raid, use Marcel's expertise to carry out an appropriate disguise, and finally have the furniture delivered directly to the room he was decorating, without it ever appearing for public sale. It was safe, and highly efficient.

Marcel brought more than commercial know-how to his Paris colleagues. Jean had been born at Melun and had remained essentially a provincial, despite his years of modest living on the Left Bank. Despite his affectations this was also true of Xavier. Claude and André both came from the suburbs, modest dormitory areas west of the capital. Marcel was a real Parisian, born in the *"Siezième"*, the most snobbish quarter of all, and brought up in an atmosphere of some sophistication. He had background, confidence, style. They were all infected by his gaiety and aware of a new sense of expansion. For too long they had lived on the cheap, stuck in the Fifth *arrondissement*, and patronised the cheap cafés at the river end of the rue de Seine, picturesque enough for tourists, but unsubstantial and unsatisfying for men in their thirties who needed to graduate to something more solid. Marcel introduced them to a new kind of society, and they were disproportionately impressed. They were all, in their different ways, happier than they had ever been before.

Xavier Richier remained apart. He did not mind Marcel dominating the syndicate in Paris, as long as they remembered that he had conceived it, organised it, and planned fifty major raids on some of the most important houses and churches in Europe. If there ever seemed any danger of their forgetting this he told them, at length. Xavier's scholarship was rare, but without Marcel the syndicate would never have developed; he provided the ideal counterpoise to the bizarre doctor who still pretended to be a disinterested disciple of beauty for its own sake. (Xavier never ceased the practice of taking a proportion of his share in objects, and not cash, but like the other members of the syndicate, he found that the more money he gained, the more he needed.)

At the time of the Dampierre theft the syndicate was operating at maximum efficiency and its prospects were excellent. Jean, Claude and André functioned as well-paid employees while Marcel acted as a kind of commercial manager. Xavier, aloof from day to day minutiae, saw himself in the role of chairman. The doctor was the syndicate's presiding genius, the grand strategist and dreamer of wild dreams, which were frequently translated into reality. He was also one of the most curious criminals of all time.

CHAPTER III

Xavier's Day Out

Until his late thirties Xavier Richier's biography was a catalogue of failure and frustration. Marcel Bihn may have been a crook but his talents were manifest. Had he decided to use his gifts legitimately he could certainly have made a brilliant, and solid, career. Xavier's eccentricities, his egomania, and his inability to work with other people, precluded the material success he had always felt was his due. And then, belatedly, he discovered that there was one rather dubious vocation which suited him ideally—stealing fine art.

It began by mistake. Isolated in the provinces he envied his younger brother's insouciant existence in the capital. In fact, Jean's life was much less glamorous than Xavier deluded himself into believing, but at this stage—in the middle fifties—the younger brother was undeniably earning his living in an area concerned with aesthetics, however marginally. Xavier's provincial practice was pure drudgery and he constantly dreamed up wild schemes offering an escape. At one point he talked of starting a restaurant in the Midi; at another he considered joining a Benedictine order as a lay brother. Finally, in 1958, Xavier had an idea that actually turned out to work in practice. He decided he would set out to learn about antiques with the eventual object of pooling such capital as he and Jean possessed to open an antique shop in Paris. Xavier began to study, attacking his chosen subject with the ferocity of a man desperate for a vocation, and also an escape route. It turned out that the unsuccessful doctor had a mind ideally suited to the pursuit of fine art: he combined rich sensuality with an unusual pleasure in the rigid intellectual discipline of artistic scholarship. Above all, he gloried in his own developing expertise. First with Jean, and later with Claude and André, he was always looking for an opportunity to point out that compared with himself they were no more than flea market judges, glorified small-time junk dealers. He spent all his spare time, and many hours that should have been dedicated to his patients, poring over reference books and catalogues, and making extensive tours of cathedrals, little known churches, museums, and above all châteaux *classés* (that is, country houses whose owners open them to the public in exchange for government subsidies). He built up an extensive library, a meticulous system of card indexing. And, very early on, he saw that great châteaux and cathedrals containing objects which might easily be as valuable as the deposits in a small-town bank were no better protected from thieves than the average suburban villa.

Eventually with Jean and his two decorator friends Xavier formed the syndicate to put this obvious insight to practical use; Marcel arrived to rationalise the thefts, like a business consultant reorganising a potentially profitable, but ill-run company. The difference between Xavier and his colleagues in Paris immeasurably complicated the task of the police, which was already difficult enough. The Paris end worked like hyper-professional criminals. When Xavier occasionally decided to steal something himself, he usually acted on impulse, though he often reconnoitred in advance. His personal speciality was small churches and a pleasant Sunday excursion he took in 1964 was typical of the Xavier Richier method.

There was something rather odd about the Renault Dauphine travelling along the cobbled road that connects Lens and Liévin —two small mining communities in the Pas-de-Calais area of Northern France. Firstly, it was driven so badly; not fast, but erratically, veering periodically from the edge of the gutter to the crown of the road. The car itself was in a state of extraordinarily advanced neglect. Originally it had been sprayed yellow.

Now the rust had so corroded the bodywork that it was nearly impossible to make out the colour at all. Dried-out mud flaked off wheels that had not been cleaned for months, years perhaps; the film of grease on the windscreen was thick enough to produce a blurred dazzle in the June sunlight. The Renault looked like the pinch-penny vehicle of a small grocer, or a harassed clerk on a meagre budget. Except that on the bottom left of the windscreen, almost obliterated by the grime, it was just possible to trace the red, spiky symbol which all doctors in France use to identify their vehicles.

Xavier was driving. He was a small man, his face pouchy, already running to fat. His scalp showed through above the hairline, his eyes were strained under their steel-rimmed glasses. The limp grey suit needed pressing; some buttons were dangling on their last thread, others had already gone. He had thrown an ancient beige raincoat on the passenger seat beside him. The weather forecast for this humid Sunday morning of June 23rd, 1964, threatened summer storms.

Xavier's erratic, preoccupied driving did not matter over the first fourteen-mile stretch of his journey, as far as Béthune. Traffic was light; this area of France does not attract visitors, even at the height of the tourist season. The cobbled road winds through the gritty suburbia of the Lens-Liévin mining complex, lined by identical rows of *corons*—brown brick terraces of miners' cottages. Only the gaunt outline of an occasional factory relieves the landscape, which is a study in oppressive monotony.

Zola deliberately chose the region for his novel *Germinal* and used harsh-grained descriptions of the mining environment to reinforce his theme—the human degeneracy which money-grubbing industrialisation had created. Nearing Béthune Xavier negotiated a crossing with signs pointing south-west to Vimy, where the French army was broken in 1915. This countryside is the historical battlefield of France. Xavier's father, who had been a young cavalry officer in 1918, would have found every name heavy with nostalgia: not so the son. He disliked all things military; indeed, organisation in any form filled him with claustrophobic distaste and he had spent most of his adult life trying to escape from it.

As a child he had endlessly been taken to barrack-square cere-

31

monials, all the more flamboyant because they were being performed by an army that had been humiliated twice in half a
century. These occasions had been intended as a treat but he
had never managed to summon up the emotions his mother and
father had expected of him. He found it all boring; he hated
the smell of the horses.

At Béthune he swung left to join the poplar-lined main road
which eventually leads to Calais. He was aiming for Aire-sur-
la-Lys, a straggling town thirteen miles out of Béthune. The
traffic was heavier now, swollen by British motorists making for
Calais. The doctor was clearly not part of the holiday-making
stream; nor was he on duty. There was no medical bag on the
front seat with his raincoat. At Aire, he by-passed the main
square and pulled up by the west wall of the Church of St.
Pierre, whose grey Gothic towers hulk over the narrow streets of
the town.

It was just after one, and the sandy forecourt of St. Pierre was
deserted. The last stragglers from mid-day Mass, girls in their
chain-store Sunday best and brilliantined boys on motor-cycles,
had gone home for lunch. The priests had retired behind the
mustard-yellow brick walls of the presbytery, thirty yards down
the side-road.

Xavier stepped out of the car and walked quickly into the
chilly church through the open door.

From the outside, St. Pierre has a certain splendour. Its main
tower is massive, and finely-modelled, and the restorations in
the sixteenth century did not spoil its character. But inside,
everything is a sorry mess. The doctor found himself standing
below a maze of garish modern statues, their blues and reds
emphasised by the violent nineteenth-century stained glass.
Halfway along the church he saw the huge white screen which
bisected the nave laterally. Behind it, the long-drawn-out post-
war restorations at which workmen from Le Havre hammered
and drilled. But not on Sundays. He walked across to the small
workmen's door at the side of the screen, and vanished.

Fifteen minutes later Xavier emerged carrying a large parcel,
wrapped in brown paper. He put it into the back of his car,
glanced around—and headed towards the centre of the town.
He did not continue far along the main road—just outside Aire

the maltreated Dauphine cut off to the right, along a small road which runs beside the river Lys. Here the river is no more than a sluggish trench, but Aire has little else to offer on a Sunday, so as usual its banks were lined with preoccupied fishermen. One or two gazed idly at the yellow Dauphine as it rattled past, swayed over the wooden bridge that crosses the railway, and took the lane that leads to the village of Boeseghem, three miles away.

Boeseghem is a farming village of fifty houses, three *estaminets*, and a chapel. Under the thick shade of a dozen oak trees, the long, gleaming gravestones of the churchyard record the generations of the peasant families who lived and died here—in isolation even from the unsophisticated metropolis of Aire. On a Sunday afternoon, Boeseghem is as still and silent as the sands of Mars; the church door stands open, the shadows edge across the gravel forecourt. The doctor's car pulled up. Once again, he went in empty-handed—and came out with a brown paper parcel. This time he was gone only minutes. The car continued its journey through the flat, dusty countryside for another two and a half miles, where it crossed a hump-backed bridge into the village of Thiennes.

Unlike Boeseghem, Thiennes has a centre—the nineteenth-century restored church of St. Eloi. The church with its un-shaded cemetery is in the exact centre of the village, forming a quadrilateral with a one-way service road following the four sides. Around the church are two *estaminets*, a minor post office and a handful of small shops, overlooking the paved forecourt which is the town's meeting place. After Mass on a summer Sunday morning (it tends to be a protracted affair, as the curé, M. Albert Noyon, likes to let his sermons run on) almost the whole population of Thiennes foregather to gossip outside the church. Only the hard-core Communists, already doing a little mild Sunday-morning drinking, stay away. But the gathering does not last very long: after half an hour or so Sunday lunch has emptied the yard. The serious drinkers take up positions in their favourite bars, against the return of the crowd around three o'clock.

The inns of Thiennes are like overgrown kitchens, decorated with plastic flowers, advertisements for Martini and hard wooden chairs. But on Sunday afternoons they provide the focus for social life, and the farmers cram in so hard that latecomers have to stand up. There are no tables outside on even the sunniest day. In this area of France, only twenty miles from the Belgian border, people prefer to take their pleasures gloomily, like the English.

The Sunday drinking tide was just beginning to flow back into the bars on June 23rd when the Dauphine appeared. In a community where the arrival of any stranger is a welcome novelty, it inevitably attracted attention, particularly when the doctor started reversing maladroitly in the wrong direction up the one-way service road. Etienne Vidal, a stolid, fresh-faced man who runs the inn opposite the west corner of the church, called his thirteen-year-old son, Daniel: "Go and tell him he's going the wrong way up a *sens unique*."

Daniel ran out—and found that the Dauphine was busy negotiating the ninety degree bend, and making a considerable mess of it. He also noticed that the plump, rumpled driver was sweating.

The Dauphine had come to rest against his own motorised bicycle, the status symbol for Thiennes teenagers, which was leaning against the wall. Daniel, aided by his seven-year-old sister Lucy, extricated his bicycle from the Renault's front bumper, checked it was undamaged, and told the driver that he ought to turn round—if he wanted to park, there was a place behind the church. The driver thanked them. The two children thought there was something funny about him. Apart from anything else, he was wearing a raincoat, and by now it was very hot.

After this moment of excitement, the citizens of Thiennes returned to their Belgian lager, and paid little attention to the man in the raincoat when he reappeared after a few minutes, this time without the car. He went into the church—and they put him down as a tourist. For Thiennes, as it happens, possesses a tourist attraction, Notre Dame de Joyel, a sixteenth-century painted wooden statue of the Virgin—in technical terms a "polychrome virgin".

Notre Dame de Joyel has a reputation for considerable intercessory powers, and although no miracles are credited to her,

she is the object of a local cult. The statue was certainly a very
fine one, although somewhat marred by a patina of dirt laid
down over years during which no irreverent cleaning had been
permitted, or probably even considered. Xavier's visit was brief.
He was not a man of religious convictions, and wasted no time
with such rituals as crossing himself, or genuflecting. The
church was completely empty.

Curé Albert Noyon, the rather autocratic priest, often has
baptisms to perform after the mid-day Mass, and tends to lunch
late in his presbytery behind the church. Afterwards he takes a
nap. Lucy Vidal, searching for something to enliven Sunday
afternoon, went for a short stroll along the pavement towards
St. Eloi, and saw Xavier leave the church. He was, she noticed,
carrying a parcel.

And that was the last that Thiennes, Aire-sur-la-Lys and
Boeseghem saw of him. He vanished completely somewhere
across the disused battlefields, the same way he had come.

Curé Noyon noticed the disappearance of Notre Dame de
Joyel shortly after six that evening. The following day, the
workmen at St. Pierre in Aire also reported an inexplicable
loss; two small chandeliers and a wooden angel. Months of
restorations in the church had left them camouflaged by dust,
effectively concealing from all but expert eyes the fact that
they were rare and important examples of seventeenth-century
ecclesiastical art. Hardly had the local policeman replaced the
telephone when yet another report came in. This time a dis-
traught curé from Boeseghem was miserably explaining that
two eighteenth-century vases, the pride of his chapel, had vanished over the weekend. The thief had chosen well because
Boeseghem is cluttered with statues and *objets,* including curiosities like the wooden side-altarpiece, painted white and gilded.
But the two vases, in clean-coloured, fresh faïence, were the only
objects of value among the jumble. It is hard to make an accurate valuation of this kind of ecclesiastical art because examples
comparatively seldom appear on the open market. A conservative evaluation of this Sunday afternoon haul would be about
£70,000. The police did their best, but never really grasped the
importance of the theft. Their confusion is understandable.

Even now it hardly seems possible that objects of this quality could have been so defenceless. No security precautions; no guards; not even a locked door. It was like shop-lifting a nine-penny comb from a chain store.

Nevertheless, they took young Daniel Vidal—the only witness who had actually spoken to the man in the beige raincoat—and showed him numerous photographs of local criminals. The boy sat in the police station at Hazebrouck staring blankly at the faces of burglars, bank robbers and petty thieves. Naturally he recognised none of them. Daniel had not noticed the half-obscured doctor's insignia on the windscreen of the Renault—but even had he done so, and reported the fact to the police, it would have made not the slightest difference. The concept of a larcenous doctor does not come easily to policemen in the French provinces. They would have assumed at once that the car must have been stolen.

In due course the Hazebrouck officers alerted their informers and checked through their list of fences, time-honoured and moderately effective ways of dealing with petty larceny. They sometimes help the detection of felons handling stolen radios, typewriters or cigarettes. But they produced no response in the case of the polychrome virgin; the two chandeliers; the vases of rare faïence; and the wooden angel.

Xavier drew up outside 6 bis, rue Thiers, a characterless bijou villa, which stands on the little town's only slight eminence (apart from its slag heaps). He was not concerned to park carefully, simply leaving the Renault with one dirty nearside wheel on the pavement, while he carried his parcels up to the first floor. The door was heavily padlocked, and when he had dealt with this there was still the mortice lock he had himself installed as a secondary defence. Finally he entered a room which appeared to have no connection with the remainder of the dingy house. When he switched the lights on its multifarious contents shone here and there with the sober brilliance of great quality and high value. Some of the objects proclaimed their class even to an inexperienced eye: a gilded miniature *fauteuil*, an armchair with the unique, floating grace conferred by the greatest chairmakers of the eighteenth century; a slender-legged writing desk patterned with infinitely delicate tendrils of marquetry. Others were more mysterious, like the strangely-patterned silk cover stitched on the bed (a very early example of silk-printing) and the dark, tattered box which the doctor's housekeeper, impatiently dusting round it (when she could be bothered) saw as just another piece of junk. It was the marriage-chest made for King Henry II of France and Diane of Poitiers in the 1560s— all the more valuable because the projected marriage never took place. It was standing on a Louis Quinze folding table elaborately patterned in spider-web marquetry, which had been in Liévin for ten months. Previously its owner, the Duc de Villefranche, had displayed it as one of his rarest possessions. A pair of heavy candle-sticks and a mediaeval statuette in dark wood had been placed on the rose-wood sideboard next to the table. The statuette was known as Notre Dame de Bon Secours, once the centrepiece of the parish church of Lieucourt in the Haute-Saône, a good 130 miles south of Liévin. The doctor had made a detour to pick it up in the course of a motor-trip to the Swiss border. It was one of his principles never to go anywhere without first listing all museums and churches *en route* in case there might be something worth removing. He found this infinitely more amusing than any conventional tourist diversions.

Xavier locked the door behind him and saw when he examined Notre Dame de Joyel, the new acquisition, that it was in woefully poor condition. He set it down so that it complemented the other mediaeval virgin. In the days that followed he worked removing the pious grime of centuries until the original colours came to life, and the knife-sharp lines of the statue's robe were once more defined as the craftsman who had carved them intended.

In the meantime the doctor fiddled about in his room finding a place for the chandeliers and the angel of St. Pierre—it finally came to rest on a child's miniature *fauteuil* which until a month earlier had figured in a collection at the Manoir de la Bouleaunnière near Fontainebleau. It was a particularly fine piece as it bore the signature of Boulard, probably the best chair-maker the eighteenth century produced.

His attachment to Fontainebleau, and its forest, was as compulsive as that of the Barbizon painters (whom, incidentally, he despised, a judgement he also applied to all nineteenth-century furniture). His own chosen period was the eighteenth century and Fontainebleau did not appeal to him because of its scenic qualities. He had acquainted himself with every side-lane in the forest because its proximity to the great palace had made it so popular as a site for eighteenth-century châteaux, minor satellites of the Court. It was very convenient that the eighteenth-century nobility's total preoccupation with Court life meant that virtually all the finest châteaux of the period were built within a day's ride of Versailles, or Fontainebleau, or Marly. This conglomeration of grand, ill-protected houses facilitated his operations enormously.

Xavier preferred to think of himself as a collector, not a thief, and certainly his passion for *haute époque* furniture (pictures interested him only mildly) was as absolute as anything great collectors of the past, Wallace, the Goncourts, or Henry Clay Frick, had felt for their chosen periods. The difference was that he had acquired his collection without spending a penny. The two examples of early *bureaux*, those writing tables with drawers fashionable at the beginning of Louis XIV's reign which stood like twins beneath his long shuttered window, had cost nothing. Neither had his four *commodes*, all signed by master furniture-makers, the chests of drawers which by the time Louis XIV was dying had largely superseded the *bureaux*, becoming simply excuses for displays of the cabinet-makers' art with no specific function. Xavier admired the Bourbons' devotion to creating extravagant beauty for its own sake, though he had no desire to emulate them. Perfection had been the criterion and the Bourbon monarchs had amassed furniture in the same spirit that primitive chieftains built up their treasure chests— as tangible demonstrations of personal wealth and glory. At the same time they knew about furniture, and had a genuine feeling for it. Louis XV had not only given his personal patronage to the finest craftsmen in Europe, he had even made his own designs to ensure that their final products were appropriate to his own glory. The doctor would have enjoyed the role of one of Louis XV's pampered craftsmen: Roentgen, Riesener, Weisweiler, Bernard van Rysen Burgh, endlessly fawned on and deferred to because of their creative skills.

Not that the late seventeenth and eighteenth centuries were the doctor's only periods. As he had shown in the course of his drive, he also regarded himself as an amateur of ecclesiastical art of the sixteenth century and earlier. He arranged the latest additions to his brilliant private museum until finally he was satisfied that they had been laid out to their best advantage. They joined the four other statues (from a church in the Pas-de-Calais); the bust of St. Innocent (the result of a trip to Douai); an unusual late mediaeval shepherd (from Fouquereuil, near Béthune); and yet another Virgin, known at Notre Dame de Salette (again from the Fouquereuil chapel). There were so many ecclesiastical objects because he had found that churches were even more vulnerable than country houses, which he would never have dreamed of trying to rob personally. He was content to ferret out choice sets of furniture in private houses and pass photographs or drawings to Claude and André.

Despite his *jeu d'esprit* that afternoon (ridiculously easy, after all) the doctor had neither the physique nor the nerve for professional house-breaking. He preferred the more contemplative role of connoisseur, directing his *"hommes de main"*—from a discreet distance. It had proved a good system. Six bis, rue Thiers was undoubtedly the most luxuriantly appointed bijou villa in Europe.

If Xavier Richier had been impudent enough to have his stolen collection valued in 1964, it would have involved a good deal of work on the part of a Lloyd's broker. He would, for instance, have needed to consult experts in at least half-a-dozen specialist areas (the expert on tapestries would have been stunned to find that the country doctor had two of the most important in Europe decorating his villa). After the broker had collated the various reports his valuation, allowing a margin to be on the safe side, would probably have been about £750,000, or roughly two million dollars.

CHAPTER IV

The Gentleman Burglar

There were only a handful of people in 1962 who were aware that northern France was in the grip of an epidemic of art thefts—not thefts of pictures, of the conventional pattern, but of fine furniture and ecclesiastical art, objects which twentieth-century thieves had previously never shown any interest in. A few senior officials in the French Cultural Affairs Ministry knew what was happening, so of course did the château owners who had lost their choicest objects, and the bishops and priests whose churches had been pillaged. But, apart from Xavier and his friends, who month by month were more convinced that they were so much smarter than the authorities that they could continue indefinitely stealing virtually anything that took their fancy, only one man had access to sufficient information to grasp how serious the situation had become.

This was a policeman, Commissaire René Chevalier, who had received a report on every art theft in France since 1960. In that year Chevalier had been appointed head of a new section of the First Paris Mobile Brigade, created expressly to deal with the theft of art. The name of his department, as grandiose as its offices in the Faubourg St. Honoré were shabby, was *Le Groupe pour la Repression du Banditisme*—the G.R.B.

By 1962 there had been approximately fifty important art thefts, almost all involving furniture stolen from large country houses. From time to time the French popular Press had tried to use these as the basis for sensational but ill-documented stories on what they had christened *"Le Gang des Châteaux"* but no one took them very seriously, least of all Chevalier who was too old a hand to let the newspapers worry him.

Now in his late forties, Chevalier had started his career on the beat in his native Normandy—riding a bicycle. From there, over a quarter of a century, he had graduated to the Paris Murder Squad, and pulled off a series of notable coups. He had no specific qualifications for his new job—Chevalier knew little about art, less about furniture, and had never been near any institution of higher education. The assumption behind the appointment was that this new kind of crime, like conventional larceny or fraud, was susceptible to traditional police methods. From the beginning Chevalier had serious reservations about this, but he largely kept them to himself.

The dossier he had inherited when he took over the job was comparatively straightforward. It revealed a wide but not very perceptive range of larceny; important pieces of furniture and statues had certainly been stolen from country houses over a period of years but almost fortuitously. In every case the thieves had wasted their energy hauling away blatant fakes and flamboyant reproductions which no serious dealer would consider. The thieves had not been art specialists but petty burglars, who had broken into châteaux in a spirit of optimism and picked up whatever happened to be lying about. Usually they would have been more profitably employed stealing television sets or cameras.

But as the Faubourg St. Honoré dossier grew thicker Chevalier began to be gravely disturbed. There was a change in the pattern of the crimes: the crooks were now more subtle, as if their student days were over, and they had graduated to the field of original research. The Commissaire, examining his reports, decided that there was only one conclusion. An organised gang of professional thieves, backed by an expert, had realised how valuable good antiques were. Fakes, reproductions and even quite important secondary pieces were ignored; the gang was concentrating on the eighteenth century, and stealing with precisely the same kind of selectivity that a rich connoisseur would employ to build up his collection. It was a dismal

41

prospect for the G.R.B. and two very similar reports which arrived in Paris during the first week of 1963 made Chevalier even more pessimistic.

For fifty-one weeks of the year Le Mans is simply an ingrown commercial town, 160 miles south-east of Paris. The fifty-second, a riotous week in June when drivers in the twenty-four-hour race, their exotic camp-followers, and over 100,000 spectators cram in, lends Le Mans certain ephemeral characteristics of a capital city. But the glamour ends with the race and the town soon eases back into its smug provincial rhythm. There are a certain number of visitors during the rest of the year, largely because Le Mans is a convenient stop-over point between Paris and the Brittany coast. The inhabitants, who speak that pure Loire Valley French which foreign students of the language are urged to copy, accept that when they come across a visitor he is almost certainly there purely by geographical accident. If one asks for sight-seeing suggestions, the reply is invariable: "The cathedral, and of course the tapestries."

These are the city's second claim to distinction. The cathedral cannot rival Chartres or Rouen but it has grandeur, and provides a fitting setting for the tapestries, which number among France's most important art treasures. They were given to the cathedral by the Cardinal of Luxembourg in 1510 and comprise five matching *tableaux*, all approximately thirty feet long and five feet high. They are exquisite examples of late mediaeval artistry, woven in liquid aquamarines and glowing golds, depicting the principal acts of the Holy Martyrs of Milan. The set is particularly unusual because of its lightness and happiness, despite the decidedly macabre subject matter. The scenes include the decapitated St. Gervais being buried by the faithful; and St. Protais and St. Gervais delivering a young girl from a demon. But the tapestries themselves, full of flowering trees and borders of roses and daisies, are marvels of decoration and meaning. They are full of detail about clothes, interior furnishings, tools and building methods—the kind of lovingly portrayed *minutiae* which fascinated the elder Breughel. They are often illustrated in French school text-books, and after the tapestry at Bayeux are the best known embroideries in France.

Their survival is something of a miracle in the light of Le Mans' violent history. In 1562 the town was captured and devastated by the Huguenots—but the tapestries were hidden. The same thing happened during the Revolution, when the Bishop of Le Mans called for help on St. Julian, the cathedral's patron saint, and then wisely embarked on a contingency plan in case St. Julian had something else on his mind. He concealed the tapestries, which survived in as perfect condition as the day when the Cardinal made his gift. And they also survived the Prussians after their defeat of Chanzy's army on the Loire in 1871, and then a further two twentieth-century world wars.

For over 100 years there has been a tradition that in the summer months the tapestries are kept in the small chapel of the Holy Sacrament where they totally cover the walls, adding perhaps a dimension for the pious (though from the point of view of the visiting art lover the light is rather poor). After the Feast of All Saints, on November 1st, they are transferred to the Gothic choir, where they remain hung round the delicate pillars until Easter. Since the middle nineteenth century this pattern had not been changed, and on November 1st 1962, as usual, the sacristan made the annual transfer, taking the five tapestries from the chapel to the choir. At nine-thirty a.m. on Saturday December 15th he was walking across the echoing stone floor on his way to the vestry. As he passed the choir he glanced casually at the tapestries hanging from the Gothic arches —to his amazement there were only four.

At first he thought it was a hallucination; and then, collecting his thoughts, decided there must be some straightforward explanation. He did nothing until the conclusion of a Mass being celebrated before a sparse collection of the faithful—mainly peasant women from the agricultural surrounds in their black shapeless dresses and head-scarves. Then he intercepted the young priest on the way to a side chapel. His excited inquiries soon confirmed that the tapestry had not been removed officially, either for cleaning or restoration work. The priest, who had come into the cathedral at seven a.m., remembered having seen all five tapestries in their normal place.

Within half an hour the cathedral was echoing with the boots of Le Mans policemen, puzzled at such an unusual crime. They got nowhere. At lunch-time the overcast skies of Le Mans opened, and the town sank under an inexorable deluge. Canon Mabon, the cathedral's most venerable priest, was weeping. By then he had discovered that the stolen tapestry was the most valuable of the set; alone of the five it carried embroidery on the back and, unknown even to most of the cathedral's priests, the signatures of the Cardinal of Luxembourg, the original donor, and also of the cathedral's most important dignitaries of the year 1510. The thief had made a discerning choice. Evidently he had embarked on detailed research.

The actual theft had been absurdly easy to carry out. Any casual visitor could have helped himself to the tapestry, on impulse even. The thief had simply strolled in after early Mass had begun, cut the ropes which fastened the tapestry to the choir, rolled it under his arm (it made a fairly bulky armful but was perfectly easy to carry), and then left the way he had come. There were no clues, and no fingerprints. It was a simple crime, but one of major importance—the tapestry could be valued at £10,000, £50,000, or indeed more or less any figure one cared to mention. It was unique, and irreplaceable.

A tapestry of equivalent quality might easily not appear on the international art market once in fifty years. Certainly the cathedral would never have considered disposing of their own set; indeed, they could not. The rarest art treasures in France, the five Le Mans tapestries among them, are classified as part of "the national patrimony". This means they cannot be sold and that the "Historic Monuments" department of the Ministry of Cultural Affairs is, theoretically, responsible both for their safe-keeping and preservation, though in the case of ecclesiastical objects the Church, not the Ministry, would normally look after its own art treasures. The Le Mans police quickly saw the implications of this. A theft of such proportions—and the absence of security arrangements to prevent it—could easily lead to some kind of critical inquest. Evidently, the Church authorities were vulnerable; the Ministry, by extension, equally so. And unless the tapestry were speedily recovered, they themselves might end up as scapegoat. The anti-Gaullist opposition, and the Press, might decide to make political capital out of the vanished tapestry. Accordingly, the Le Mans prefecture prudently shunted the case on to Paris as rapidly as seemed decent.

Within days their colleagues at Laval, a provincial town twenty-five miles away, found themselves in a similarly painful situation. On Christmas Eve, Monsieur Valier, verger of the Basilica of Avesnieres, Laval's most important church, walked his habitual sixty yards from the presbytery in the rue de l'École to the small, tree-bordered square overlooking the river Mayenne, where the Basilica has stood since the end of the twelfth century. Building was continued in the thirteenth and fourteenth centuries, and the structure as a whole restored— rather insensitively—in the nineteenth. Since then it has fallen into decay.

Valier entered the Basilica via the porch, paradoxically the best kept section of the church with its exhortatory posters about communion classes, "Your Child is looking for a Direction in Life", and parish notices. He walked up the east aisle towards the altar, stopping for a moment to have a word with a friend he saw in the transept, the most ancient part of the church, built in 1170. It was a fortunate conversation because he happened to glance towards the confessional boxes on the south side of the transept and noticed something odd. His emotions were very like those of the sacristan in the Le Mans cathedral a week earlier.

Between the confessional boxes there was a white patch on the wall, about four feet from the ground and roughly ten feet long. It stood out as if someone had painted a white square on the dingy, grey brickwork. Valier realised at once that the white patch was in fact the area normally covered by the only object of value in the Basilica—their Louis XIII Aubusson tapestry depicting a scene from the Old Testament.

Valier was puzzled. The tapestry had hung in that spot for generations; presumably it must have been removed for cleaning. Christmas Eve seemed an odd time to choose. He was irritated that this should have been done without his knowing, and he went to make inquiries. He first asked Curé Marain, who had been hearing Christmas confessions. When Marain knew nothing about it he tried all the other priests in turn— even making a special journey back to the presbytery in search of information. There was none.

It did not take long to establish that the Laval tapestry had gone the same way as the one from Le Mans. This time there was even less information about the theft; no one remembered definitely having seen the tapestry later than the previous Saturday. Perhaps the Le Mans thief had tried his hand a second time. One of the priests remembered having exchanged a few words at the beginning of the week with a neatly dressed man in his early thirties who had spent at least an hour in the church. The encounter had only lasted a couple of minutes, but stuck in his mind because the man had said he was professionally interested in the Basilica as he worked for the "Beaux Arts" department of the Louvre, a section of which, the Historic Monuments department, was responsible for the Laval tapestry, as well as the set at Le Mans. Unfortunately, because of the habitual gloom inside the Basilica, the priest was able to give only the vaguest description of the stranger. Yes, he spoke with an educated voice. Yes, he was about thirty. No, he was clean-shaven, or had he perhaps a small moustache . . . ? It soon became clear, even to the local police, that the old man did not really remember very clearly—after all, there had been no reason why he should have subjected the young stranger to an intense scrutiny. There were no other leads, no further information of any kind. For forty-eight hours they conducted a desultory investigation leading nowhere. Apart from anything else, the police failed to see why anyone should want to steal a dirty old tapestry. If they had been told that certain art collectors would have regarded £20,000 as a bargain price for it, they would have thought it a joke. In the end they reacted in the same fashion as their colleagues at Le Mans. They shrugged uncomprehendingly at the unfathomable oddities of the criminal classes, hurried off a memorandum to Paris, and thankfully consigned their meagre dossier on the affair to a back shelf.

Chevalier read the additions to his dossier uneasily. The tapestry reports were in many ways similar to the pile he had already acquired on châteaux thefts. The thieves had demonstrated the same expertise and ability to select; the local police seemed helpless, and as usual there was the gentlest implication between the formal lines of their report that they were already too hard-pressed coping with *real* crimes to embark on a major investigation in this arcane area. Undoubtedly, the Le Mans theft was the most important yet, a fact which had a certain depressing logic about it. He might have guessed the thieves would turn their attention to major works of ecclesiastical art. French churches are even easier to steal from than French country houses.

But there was a new, puzzling fact, which Chevalier raised with his two senior assistants, Inspectors Louis Raton and Joseph le Bruchec. They had all been brought up on an axiom of police work: the most complex crime invariably becomes comprehensible once its motive has been isolated. Until now all the art thefts had been characterised by a clean economic rationale—there are always people eager to buy antique furniture of the highest quality, so eager that they might not bother over-much where it had come from. But the Le Mans tapestry was in a quite separate category. Where, conceivably, could a thief sell it?

The three detectives had learnt a good deal about antiques since they had joined the G.R.B. but they did not delude themselves that they were real experts. Chevalier telephoned Jacques Dupont, Director-General of the Historic Monuments department, who is one of Europe's leading connoisseurs, as well as a gifted civil servant. Where could the Le Mans tapestry be sold?

Dupont had no hesitation. Nowhere. He added that it would be like trying to sell the Mona Lisa at the Hotel Drouot or the British Crown Jewels in Bond Street. There was no explanation of the theft, then? Chevalier asked. Dupont then made an apparently flippant remark, which turned out to be crucial. "The newspapers will probably find one. Doubtless, they will start talking about a mad collector . . ."

The two agreed that any such idea was absurd, the kind of fantasy they had read about as boys in the Arsène Lupin adventures. Lupin, the nonchalant hero of a phenomenally successful series of detective stories published before the Great War, is the French equivalent of Raffles. Generations of French schoolboys have been brought up on the adventures of this master criminal whose speciality was the theft of art treasures, partly because he was a connoisseur, and partly because it amused him to outwit the police. The most famous book of the series was called *Arsène Lupin—Gentleman Cambrioleur,* meaning the Gentleman Burglar. Chevalier found that the phrase had stuck in his mind.

But there were other things to think about. Where had the thieves disposed of the considerable quantity of important furniture already stolen (so far, the police had regained nothing important)? How were they able to make such decisive and expert selections, removing a few superlative pieces and ignoring other objects which to the police, indeed to anyone not a gifted connoisseur, appeared of equally fine quality? Most important of all, what kind of a gang was it that managed to combine the technique of professional criminals with the very different skills of a top antique dealer?

Every evening at six-thirty René Chevalier was in the habit of closing his office for the night, descending to the ground floor in the Heath Robinson Edwardian lift, and spending a contemplative hour seated on a yellow *banquette* in the bar conveniently adjoining the G.R.B.'s headquarters—"Le Regal".

Here "Le Patron", as his G.R.B. team called him, would listen impassively to their daily assessments, chain-smoking acrid Gitanes in rice-paper and lubricating his mental processes with a classic Marseilles pick-me-up—Ricard 51 laced with Grenadine and half an inch of iced water. The evening after the Laval report had arrived Chevalier mystified Raton and le Bruchec by introducing an unaccustomed literary element into the conversation.

As a parting shot before leaving for his home in the northern suburbs he ordered them to read a book—*Arsène Lupin—Gentleman Cambrioleur,* the old thriller classic. And then, without explaining why, he ambled out of the glass doors into the Faubourg.

CHAPTER V

The Respectable Family Richier

They were never a lucky family but their beginnings were auspicious enough. Soon after the Great War a strikingly pretty, rather pampered blonde called Pauline Rocques fell in love with Etienne Richier, a young cavalry officer. He had already seen action, at the very end of the war the French call "Quatorze-Dixhuit"; it was lucky for him that it had been at the end, or he would almost certainly have numbered among the casualties of Verdun or the Somme offensives. As it was he lived to fight another war, and the 1918 armistice saw him at the outset of his military career.

His regiment, the Second Chasseurs, was fashionable; but Etienne, an unexceptional young man from an unexceptional family, had one thing very much against him—he had no fortune. The Rocques were rich, and the head of the family, Georges Rocques, was a scholar and scientist with an international reputation for his work in experimental chemistry. They regarded themselves as intellectuals. This reason alone, apart from Etienne's lack of money, was enough to create opposition to the marriage. Pauline was warned that she was exchanging an interesting (and even elegant) social background for the colourless round of a peace-time officer's wife. Army officers, they said, would bore her to distraction. Pauline was not prepared to listen; she was in love.

The marriage turned out badly in various ways and the fact

49

that her family's gloomy prophecies were fulfilled made her all the more bitter. For his part Etienne found peace-time soldiering a frustrating and financially unrewarding métier. There was one brief transformation of their lives when he was posted to North Africa, and they were both able to enjoy the artificially high standards of the French *colon* society which turned every administrator into a temporary aristocrat. They expanded and relaxed—at last their way of life began to approximate to their aspirations. Pauline adored colonial privilege. It didn't last.

This section of Etienne's career became a family fable and the children were brought up on tales of sun and sea, elegant garden parties and devoted servants—Pauline described this golden age so often that Xavier and his younger brother Jean found it impossible to separate things they really remembered happening from their mother's nostalgic evocations. Xavier, born in 1922, was old enough to have genuine childhood memories of Algiers. Jean, the second brother, who had been born with his twin sister at Melun in February 1929, was not— but this did not stop him telling friends that he had been brought up in North Africa. He probably even believed it was true. Xavier, even more than his younger brother, found that the weight of family nostalgia had left him with a life-long obsession. As a man in his forties he still frequently told people that one day he would return for ever to North Africa, the one society with which he truly felt in sympathy. He would build a house in Algeria or Morocco and dedicate himself to the pursuit of beauty.

However, over a period of more than thirty years, the Richier family destiny propelled them farther and farther north. Etienne was transferred from Algiers to Sedan, the archetype of those dreary garrison towns Pauline's family had described when trying to kill the marriage. For a century it has formed the core of France's military defence against Germany—a grey, cold city full of grandiose public monuments, most of which, when one examines them, turn out to be commemorating notable defeats. Pauline hated it. While she played listless rubbers of bridge with other officers' wives, she dreamt of Paris. Xavier, and in due course Jean, both attended the Sedan Lycée;

50

neither demonstrated more than mediocre academic gifts. When war came, life had settled into a drab provincial pattern.

But Etienne was happy. He was promoted from Commandant to Lt.-Colonel and he began to recall his dashing youth as a Cavalry subaltern. Like all French professional soldiers his memories of "Quatorze-Dixhuit" had become rose-tinted; after a twenty year gap it now seemed like a proud record of great victories. But the Richiers' cycle of bad luck was firmly set. Etienne's regiment was virtually wiped out in one of the first engagements of the war, and he himself captured. Pauline, trying to cope with war-time severities, spent the next four years in Sedan, receiving sporadic letters marked with the "offlag" stamp of Etienne's military camp. Then the Richier's daughter, Jean's twin sister, died. And in 1944 Etienne was transferred to an officers' camp in Hamburg, only three hours by train away from his family. It seemed that the German capitulation would come at any time and they would be reunited, but the pattern of evil luck held—Etienne was killed in a British raid on Hamburg, the last of the war.

From then on Pauline relied more and more on Jean, turning to him for feminine comfort. The strain on the family began to tell; after 1944 they all developed nervous symptoms of one kind or another. The mother suffered from migraine and periods of acute anxiety bordering on complete nervous prostration. Xavier, a short-sighted, ungainly young man, tended increasingly to detach himself from his mother and brother, but never succeeded in making any close friends. Jean had developed a bad stammer and started on a long course of speech therapy. He never entirely lost a curious lisp, and he used exaggeratedly rolled "r"s which his Paris friends found amusing and put down to a mixture of affectation and a Burgundian accent he had picked up during one of the family's numerous military postings.

The Richiers were now entirely dependent on a widow's pension but rents at least were comparatively cheap; Pauline was able to satisfy one of her long-held ambitions. After a quarter of a century she moved back to Paris, acquiring an apartment in the Place Léon-Blum and preparing to devote herself entirely to her sons. By now grey-haired but always immaculately dressed, she was still very much the Colonel's wife and she set herself up as stylishly as she could manage. Her home, not far from the Place de la Bastille, is in a socially ambiguous section of Paris, a sea of tough proletarianism in which one or two islands of bourgeois respectability survive. The Place Léon-Blum is one of them, a mixture of motor-car showrooms, cafés and slightly down-at-heel blocks of apartments which had pretensions when they were built fifty years ago. The Richiers moved into number six, and Xavier, without any particular aptitude, studied as a medical student and eventually succeeded in qualifying. Medicine never inspired him, although a brief course at the Hospital St. Anne in Paris gave him an interest in psychiatry (which he never followed up). As soon as his thesis —on streptomycin—was accepted by the French Medical Council in 1952, he set up a confident brass plate—"Xavier Richier, Medecin Diplomé de Paris"—outside his mother's flat, and waited for the customers to flock in. At this period they both had visions of Xavier creating a fashionable Paris practice. Unfortunately, although Xavier was adequately competent, he lacked charm. French doctors with successful private practices have a tendency to dress and behave as if they are diplomats from the Quai d'Orsay. After several depressing months, Xavier and his ambitious mother were forced to accept that without the capital to purchase an already established practice—the equivalent of at least £10,000—the process of building one up from scratch was beyond him. He needed a regular pay-check, and quickly. The best position going turned out to be with that peculiarly French institution, the Sapeurs Pompiers of Paris.

From Xavier's point of view the job had one advantage. Apart from his affection for his mother he was an ardent misogynist, and one of the greatest barriers in launching his private practice had been his lack of assurance with women patients. (As a student he had found gynaecology highly distasteful; later in his medical career he was to refuse to examine women patients under any circumstances.) His new situation meant that women patients would be rare.

The S.P. are a corny French joke, filling the equivalent role in innumerable dirty stories to the commercial traveller in England, or the iceman in America. But they take themselves very seriously indeed, and are particularly eloquent on the sub-

ject of their own history which began in the year 1810 when
the Austrian Embassy was gutted in one of Paris's most famous
fires. The Emperor Napoleon, who had little faith in civilian
institutions, promptly decided that fire-fighting was too important to be trusted to any one but soldiers. He therefore created
a municipal fire-fighting brigade with army training and discipline, though working for the civil authorities.

At least the 2nd Chasseurs had possessed a certain anachron-
istic social cachet and had worn brilliant uniforms; the Sapeurs
Pompiers, determinedly military though they were, had no such
marginal consolations. Xavier arrived every morning at Métro
Port-Royal (he was still too badly paid to afford a car) and made
his disconsolate way 100 yards up the Boulevard to Number 55,
the brown-brick, only too clearly military headquarters squat-
ting hideously on the left-hand side. A sentry, in denims,
guarded the gate; by eight a.m. when Xavier was expected to
start his day, batches of brawny recruits, also in blue denim,
were performing obscure drill routines in the courtyard, bel-
lowing their numbers in turn and rolling lengths of white hose.
Above Richier there was a Captain-Doctor, a Colonel-Doctor,
and ultimately a General-Doctor. As one of the eleven young
doctors on the staff he was on call twenty-four hours a day. He
found the discipline irksome, the atmosphere drab. It was all
extremely remote from the elegant Parisian world which Xavier
liked to think about (and imagine himself in)—the *Tout Paris*
which consists of perhaps 2,000 people and stresses its exclusiv-
ism by its nickname suggesting that the other eight million or
so don't exist. Xavier was one of the eight million.

Later in life he tried to impress provincial acquaintances with
myths of a glittering life in intellectual Parisian society, but on
another occasion he contradicted himself with a more honest
remark.

"The period with the Sapeurs Pompiers was drudgery," he
told his locum. "It was the most I could do to find time to have
a cup of coffee."

It was only a matter of time before he found another job; it
turned out to be medical officer attached to the Miners' Welfare
Centre in the Lens-Liévin coalfields. It was far from being a
prize situation but after the Sapeurs Pompiers interlude he was

ready to grasp at anything. At first he was delighted by the
release from para-military discipline and the fact that now, for
the first time, he was sufficiently well-paid to afford a car. He
also enjoyed the prestige, but none of these minor satisfactions
proved lasting. He seemed to be trapped; his personal history,
and that of his family over a period of forty years, had acquired
an inexorable, cyclical quality of the kind that so appealed to
the French post-Edwardian novelists he had read, without much
enthusiasm, at the Sedan Lycée.

Ironically, Xavier's own biography seemed to be running ever
more in parallel with that of his father—a pattern he had always
sworn to avoid. Like Etienne, Xavier found himself frozen in an
institutional structure, humourless, rigid, inimical to individu-
ality. Like him, he was leading a repetitive provincial existence
in northern France; again like him, he had reached a state of
such overpowering frustration that he was ready to follow any
escape route. For Etienne it had been the Second World War;
for his son, a wild anarchic course which he deceived himself
into believing was a reasonable, even inspired means of burst-
ing out of his constriction.

The Liévin doctor had learnt that he could not win, according to the prevailing rules; he therefore decided to create a new
set for himself. A moment's self-examination would have
revealed how irrationally he was behaving but he was in the
grip of a mania. His was the last, bleak gamble of a desperate
man, a temperamental loser. But after so many years of failure
and frustration, everything seemed to be going right. At last he
was dominating his environment; perhaps he had developed into
a habitual winner. Xavier, after caution in the early days of the
gang when they had stolen not simply for money, and without
realising how far they could progress, was happier than ever
before.

CHAPTER VI

The Liévin Château

"The road stretched ahead towards Marchiennes with its two leagues of cobblestones, running dead straight through the reddish earth like a greasy ribbon . . . These roads in the Nord, running straight as a die from one manufacturing town to another, or with slight curves and gentle gradients, are turning into a single industrial city. The little brick houses, colourwashed to make up for the climate, some yellow, some blue, but others black (perhaps so as to reach the ultimate black with the least delay), ran down hill, twisting to right and left. Here and there the line of little huddled façades was broken by a large two-storeyed house, the home of some manager. A church, built of brick like everything else, looked like some new type of blast furnace, with its square tower already black with coal-dust. But what stood out most of all among the sugar refineries, rope-works and sawmills, was the immense number of dance-halls, bars, and pubs—there were over five hundred of them to a thousand houses."

Emile Zola's description, in *Germinal*, of the Lens-Liévin area still holds good, seventy years after he wrote it. This industrial complex, based on coal-mining, and spreading as far as Arras and Béthune, is perhaps the ugliest landscape in France. It seems like another country, and indeed nearly is, being almost astride the Belgian border. Liévin is nearer Dover than

55

Paris; Watney's Red Barrel beer signs gleam outside the innumerable bleak bars. Spiritually Liévin is akin to the English Black Country or the great American coalfields. People are ingrown and wary of strangers; the legacy of poverty, as well as two wars, hangs heavily over the place. The French mines have long formed an industrial ghetto for the least privileged members of society. The young people have only one ambition—to get away, preferably to Paris, which is discussed as if it were a fabled city of another continent. Many young people do leave. Who is left to work the mines? Every day there are queues of North Africans, the new under-privileged, waiting impassively at the Lens railway station for the coach to take them towards the slag-heaps.

By the end of 1952, when Dr. Xavier Richier, Diplomé de la Faculté de Médecine de Paris and former medical officer to the Sapeurs Pompiers, arrived to take up his new post, Zola's desolate prophecy about the area's development had been comprehensively fulfilled. The five-mile square Lens-Liévin complex was now one industrial city; it had been so heavily built up that patches of field or even grass were a rarity, and one could drive for a mile without seeing a tree. Yet the flat plain with only slag heaps to provide grim, sporadic, contours could not truly be described as a city. It was, and is, a sprawl of proletarian suburbs without soul or centre, boundaries, beginning or end.

The whole development is a successful exercise in nihilism. Lens and Liévin melt indistinguishably into one another with the completeness sometimes achieved in a marriage between nonentities. Liévin has little to offer even the mildest sophisticate. Such night life as exists revolves round two cafés; one, "Les Cendriers", is appropriately named as it faces the town's red-cindered main square, giving clients a view of unparalleled desolation. There is also "Le Club Karting". Here, as the name suggests, the "sporting" element meet to drink Red Barrel and compare carburettors. "Le Karting" with its mixture of French provincial status symbols (juke-box; plastic stools; and bamboo walls) clearly has the edge in glamour, but by ten-thirty its blinds are down. Ask for the gastronomic speciality of the area, and after some hesitation they tell you "soup". A culinary guide to the area might well be called "Frites with Everything". A shabby beige bus connects Lens and Liévin, but the last one leaves Liévin at eight-thirty in the evening. On Saturday night there is an extension until ten; then the local pop group, called "Les Frenetiques", perform in the Salle Tabourin.

But for the moment at least Xavier Richier did not fully realise what he had let himself in for. All he could think of was that he was going to be paid well enough to afford a car, and that he had finally put the Sapeurs Pompiers behind him. But Xavier soon, inevitably, came to hate Liévin. The only part of the north he liked was the château country of the Ile de France —he was haunted by images of grand houses surrounded by lavish lawns, their interiors embellished with delicate fantasies in gold and wood designed to titillate the rich. Now he was by no means badly paid (by 1960 he was earning £3,500 a year with a rent-free house thrown in), but he was still far from being rich. What really upset him was the lack of educated people to share his own cultivated interests—apart from a handful of mining engineers and technicians the area supports no bourgeoisie. There are a few commercial aristocrats: successful shopkeepers and garage owners.

Curé Bernaud, the local priest, lived a couple of hundred yards from Xavier, and got to know him well during his thirteen years in Liévin.

"There is not a lot here for a man of his tastes. I'm afraid the atmosphere is degenerate." After fourteen years' experience, Bernaud describes his own disillusionment with some passion: "I'm broken down by the Reds, and the alcoholism; three litres of wine a day is reckoned to be normal. I sometimes think those members of my flock who are not alcoholic are all adulterers."

Bald except for a wild fringe of hair on either side of his head, the priest wears an expression of defeat beneath his unkempt eyebrows. Xavier soon acquired the same look. He settled down in the house the nationalised mining company allocated him at 6 bis, rue Thiers. There are five rooms on two floors, and just under half an acre of garden. The Richier garden soon became a chaos of weeds, and from time to time the doctor's neighbours suggested he should hire someone to clean it up.

"He told me to mind my own affairs, very grossly," said the

indignant lady who lives opposite. "There was obviously something very peculiar about the man."

As time passed he became increasingly eccentric; his isolation
in a sea of ugliness began to obsess him, and as far as is possible
for a doctor, Xavier Richier turned into a recluse. "Why should
I talk to people unless it is absolutely unavoidable?" he asked
the priest. "This is a society of philistines."

There were, however, some advantages. Xavier's life, as seen
by his Liévin neighbours, was rather odd, sometimes downright
peculiar, but never suspicious. No one got any hint that his
activities were criminal; and Liévin, an apparently ill-advised
choice, turned out to be a perfect camouflage. Perhaps the most
important advantage was the considerable status attached to
being one of the few professional men in the community. As a
doctor Xavier could, and indeed did, get away with virtually
anything, and by the end of his period in Liévin he had arrived
at a point where he made few concessions to the outside world
at all. For instance, his driving was appalling—frequently he
did not even bother to *park* his yellow Renault Dauphine; he
just got out and walked away leaving the car in the middle of
the road, or diagonally across the pavement. But the police never
dared to disturb him. (According to an often repeated local
anecdote, another doctor in the area is said to have escaped without even a reprimand from an incident in which, driving his
car while drunk, he knocked a man down and killed him.)

The work which Xavier took on was far from demanding. He
presided from nine to eleven each morning at the mine dispensary and surgery, three minutes' drive from his house. During the afternoon he might make a few visits—and that was all.
A doctor in general practice in France can make considerably
more money than the mining company pays. But it would be
hard for any doctor with Xavier's unenthusiastic approach to
the practice of medicine to be better rewarded for effort ex-
pended.

He found the 2,500 miners for whom he was responsible
notably unsympathetic—a feeling which they reciprocated—
and none of the neighbouring doctors, including even Edouard
Westeel, his colleague and successor, ever managed to sustain
any discussion with him about medical theory or practice. If

such a subject came up in conversation, Xavier would walk away. Again, most doctors try at least to glance through the mass of literature which comes to them from drug houses and research establishments, to keep as far as possible up to date with new methods of treatment. Richier simply burnt all the literature which came to the house.

His diagnostic techniques were also decidedly individual. Even in a town where, as in most mining communities, the major disease was silicosis, he generally refused to sound people's chests with the stethoscope. He was always reluctant to conduct physical examinations. When he visited patients in their homes, he used to trot round the room examining pieces of furniture ("Where did you get this? Did your grandfather leave it to you?") and would make only cursory inquiries about the patient's health. Colleagues who took over his practice when Xavier went on holiday were often annoyed that he showed no interest in the progress of his patients when he came back.

Liévin had a bad effect on him; any psychiatrist who had seen him in his last years would almost certainly have thought his behaviour suggested a need for treatment. But though he sometimes infuriated his associates beyond patience—the occasion when he gave a rare dinner-party and at the last moment rushed into a neighbour's garden and stripped it of flowers to provide a table decoration will never be forgotten—he also became a welcome source of colour and gossip in a society where the human features are as monochrome as the skyline. He developed into something of a licensed jester, and sometimes a butt. In December 1964, for example, the local doctors gave their annual Ball of Sainte-Barbe, a continuation of the medical students' post-examination celebration, in Liévin's Salle Tabourin. One of the high spots of the evening came when another doctor, a muscular comedian, lifted Xavier off his feet and deposited him, kicking and squealing, on top of a high table. Xavier accepted it in good part. His airy, fantastic style would have been a little ornate even for a reasonably sophisticated *haut bourgeois* background. In Liévin, it produced only incomprehension, or surprisingly virulent animosity.

Xavier's casualness extended, for the most part, to his domestic arrangements. His Polish housekeeper, Solange Pridatek, a fat and gloomy woman with iron-grey hair, was devoted to him, but rather less attached to the standard household virtues; in her time the house was bathed in a rich, Gothic gloom. Xavier ate in the kitchen, usually out of tins. Only two people in Liévin established a relationship with him: Dr. Westeel and Curé Bernaud. They neither shared his tastes nor understood his eccentricities, but they extended him a measure of slightly puzzled tolerance. To these friends, Xavier was capable of generosity and consideration. Curé Bernaud, for instance, is now advanced in his sixties, and in poor health. Xavier was remarkably patient with his many symptoms, and in a moment of inspiration presented him with a boxer dog. "Ever since my dog came," says the curé, "I've slept at nights like a butterfly."

Bernaud was also grateful to Xavier for paying 500 new francs (£40) for a lamp, which he sold to him at Xavier's request. And it was Xavier, whom the curé describes as *"croyant, mais non pratiquant"* (a believer, but not a practising one), who gave the church a Louis XIV collection bag in leather, which is still used, "though I have to admit it is not ideal for the purpose."

Xavier's interest in churches was more academic than spiritual and he was never seen at Mass (except occasionally when his mother was down for the weekend). The curé's church has no aesthetic pretensions, apart from the Louis XIV souvenir; true to the depersonalised traditions of the place it is known simply as "The Church of Sector Three".

Xavier liked to give presents to these pathetically few friends; he also enjoyed talking to them at great length; he specialised in scandal, office politics in the mining corporation, and stories of his holidays, which were usually spent in North Africa. His African reminiscences were picaresque and unlikely—even the youngest athlete could not have performed in the (male) brothels of Tunis with the prowess claimed by Xavier. He once came near to a serious indiscretion by making an extraordinary offer to a local journalist at Lens, when he proposed to write an article for the principal local newspaper, *La Voix du Nord*, outlining his experiences in the Tunis *maisons de tolerance*— by no means the kind of copy this sober little journal is accustomed to run.

After his frequent absences from Liévin Xavier would chatter

to Westeel and Bernaud about *louche* nights in Paris. He enjoyed teasing the curé; one weekend, he assured him, he would
initiate the venerable cleric into the delights of a transvestite
night-club in Paris of which he was a member. This became a
standing joke. "It would hardly be appropriate for me to appear
wearing my soutane," the priest would say. "Entirely the reverse, my dear curé. You would enjoy an outstanding and
memorable success."

However, most of it was fiction. The doctor's emotional energies were concentrated on felony, and on his collection. The
homosexual escapades were a cover; it could have been clear to
anyone observant that the doctor led a double life, and that
he preferred his acquaintances to believe that his oddities—the
sudden and frequent departures, the *chic* he cultivated when
outside Liévin—could be explained by his sexual tastes. The
cover worked extremely well.

Westeel noticed that despite his unkempt appearance in
Liévin the doctor possessed an extensive wardrobe of well-
tailored suits, silk shirts and ties, and hand-made shoes that he
reserved for those days when he was going out of town, usually
to Paris; but he never asked himself how Xavier could afford
them. For these trips Westeel or some other local doctor would
often be co-opted to drive the peacock Xavier to the station at
Lens or Arras—and help carry his large, and invariably heavy
suitcases. His reluctance to travel, even for the weekend, without a great collection of bags, was a joke among his friends. On
one occasion the exploited Westeel complained that one trunk
was so heavy it must surely contain a corpse. Xavier was un-
amused.

Over a period of roughly two years at the end of the 1950s
the doctor lived in a state of perpetual tension and anxiety. He
hated strangers visiting the house, and gave his patients instructions that they must never call there without a prior telephone message. The villa was guarded like an army strongpoint.
Indeed, the heavy white shutters with padlocks which he had
installed on all the ground-floor windows were the only con-
tribution to the upkeep of the Welfare Society's property that
Xavier ever made.

Apart, that is, from the elaborate anti-burglar systems installed, rather to the amusement of his friends, on the private rooms upstairs. Everyone knew that the doctor was a collector, who took excessive pride in his old things. It was thought to be another example of his eccentricity and perverse objection to being the same as other people. Liévin's centre possesses a large group of shops entirely dedicated to disposing of the latest "contemporary styled" furniture and pastel-shaded household appliances on deferred payment schemes. Just as Xavier despised the nineteenth- and twentieth-century contributions to the decorative arts, his patients and friends equally hated anything "old-fashioned". It was typical of the man, they thought, that he did not so much as own a television set—the *sine qua non* of material respectability—and yet cared so much about dusty old chairs that on one occasion he shouted at the unfortunate Curé Bernaud for lowering his fourteen stone into a *fauteuil* which for some reason had found its way into the downstairs living-room.

Apart from occasional discoveries in the houses of his patients the doctor bought few items locally. Neither Lens nor Liévin boasts an antique shop between them, but some way out of Lens, on the monotone road to Lille, are the small premises of Madame Tosca. Her shop is not grand, but she sometimes acquires odd pleasant items of furniture, usually country-style, from sales at farm houses in the area. Small-time Paris dealers, often from St. Ouen, make a habit of calling on her in the course of their provincial tours and so, in the late fifties, did Xavier Richier. At the very beginning it was clear to this agreeable lady, who came originally from Bologna, that the doctor did not know what he was talking about in the field of antiques. And, naturally, he talked a lot. He once even bought a pair of ormolu candle-sticks from her, *circa* 1840, and later assured her that she had made a serious mistake—they were certainly much earlier. But later she noticed that his early amateurishness as a collector had changed. "He would rattle off hall-marks and the *estampilles* of the *ébénistes* like a parrot. Once or twice he was able to advise me about things I'd bought without knowing exactly what they were but he no longer ever made an offer for anything himself. I supposed he must have found a better source of supply."

It was an understatement worthy of a British diplomat. But Madame Tosca noticed that while his knowledge had deepened his manners had not improved; if anything he was more supercilious and conceited than ever. The difference, also noted by Bernaud and Westeel, was that now his arrogance no longer seemed the result of shyness, indeed the fear of other people. By 1962 he had convinced himself that he was superior to virtually everyone he ever met. Xavier Richier had adopted what he regarded were the airs of an eighteenth-century aristocrat as a complement to his personal achievement—the secret re-creation in his ordinary villa of the leisured *haute époque* style. In a sense he had turned 6 bis, rue Thiers into the nearest equivalent of a grand château that Liévin will ever see. And he wanted to play at being lord of his manor.

CHAPTER VII

Cocktails at Ménars

With the Liévin doctor and his curious Parisian associates growing more confident all the time, René Chevalier foresaw a situation—in his more pessimistic moments—where the art thefts
could pose a serious threat to every cathedral, country house,
and museum in France. Yet, it seemed, he was making no progress; the thieves came and went as they wished, leaving no
trace. The provincial police forces had neither the resources,
nor the expertise, to make more than cursory investigations.
Virtually none of the stolen furniture was ever recovered, apart
from odd pieces found by chance and providing no lead back
to the thieves.

Xavier's obsessional mind directly inspired the thefts, but
there was also an external factor. The laws of criminal economics have a kind of Marxist certainty about them. Almost every
decade produces its own minor variations of crime, and as the
Western economy evolves, so the varieties of crime available to
the anti-social multiply. The facilities for rape, for instance,
have been with us for a long time, but it has only recently become possible to commit airline ticket frauds. Each extension of
the credit system, the cheque, the credit card, multiply the possibilities of fraud, one of the two classic crimes of the twentieth
century. Art robbery is the second—including everything from
paintings to jewellery. But the sort of art robbery which
appeared in France in the 1960s was a new class of crime, or
at least a clearly defined and original subdivision of an existing

64

category. Just as credit cards began by creating a series of variations on the theme of the dud cheque, until they made cheque frauds virtually obsolete, so the general increase in antique prices, and particularly of eighteenth-century objects, suggested a simple alternative to the art thief. It was no longer necessary to attack famous (and well guarded) masterpieces. Given the required equipment, which was nothing more than erudition, (admittedly a rare criminal accomplishment) an immense profit could be made by pillaging the lesser-known and almost freely available treasures of the countryside. It is only surprising that a gang equipped to pursue such a scheme on a grand scale did not come into existence earlier, because the situation that provided the economic rationale for their activities had existed at least since the middle fifties when art prices reached a plateau. From then on, any serious collection of furniture was a natural target for people of easy moral scruple who reckoned that bank robbery was too dangerous and difficult. In the years after the war, antique furniture prices were artificially low; by 1950 they had started to recover, and after that they rose every year. The turning point, perhaps, was the price of £20,245 for a Louis XV writing table by Bernaud van Riessen Burgh in 1956. Next year a commode was sold in New York for £17,500, confirming a trend that the more percipient international dealers had been anticipating for some time. It was soon clear to everyone that this was no false boom.

The Groupe pour la Repression du Banditisme was created in 1960 and it was not a coincidence that the same year also saw a new peak of price levels for eighteenth-century furniture. At different sales, an Oeben work table went for £13,650; a gueridon table by Carlin for £12,850; a green commode for £18,375; and, incredibly, Marie Antoinette's dog-kennel for £6,425. Thieves with the necessary erudition, and resources for disposing of the stolen antiques, were well placed to make a quick and easy fortune.

Chevalier had only to flick through his voluminous files to see the new sophistication the gang had acquired. A comparison between two raids, the first in June 1961, the second eighteen months later, shows how they developed.

*   *   *

In the second week of June every year Comte Robert de Dampierre is invariably to be found at the Chantilly race-course, which he modestly describes as "the nearest French equivalent to Ascot". An easy-going man, who has always found Irish thoroughbreds more gripping than eighteenth-century furniture, he has a pleasant château (not connected with the Dampierre owned by the Duc de Luynes) at Coulanges in the Eure, roughly 120 miles west of Paris. Because a young English girl was staying with the family in June 1961, he good-naturedly sacrificed his race meeting and took her instead for an expedition to see his country house. The Comtesse de Dampierre does not collect antiques seriously, but is much more interested than her husband in those the family have acquired over the years. When they arrived at the house on a sunny Saturday afternoon, the Comtesse entered ahead of the others. She found a large bed, a lamp, and a night table in the middle of the hall. She started to complain, assuming her sons had been down to Coulanges, held a party, and left everything in a mess. Gradually she realised they had been burgled.

But the Dampierres had been lucky, entirely because of the thieves' ignorance. The family possessed, for instance, one signed commode, worth at least £4,000. The thieves left it behind. Instead they took a second chest more highly polished than the first, which they obviously thought was more valuable. In fact, it was worth less than half as much. All the occasional tables had gone, probably because they were easy to carry. The Dampierres were fond of them but they had no particular value.

The thieves also wasted their time and energy on some nineteenth-century vases, which would scarcely have covered the cost of hiring a van, but they did remove, presumably by mistake, a pair of fine *famille Rose* vases, worth approximately £1,000. The Château de Coulanges contained about fifty chairs. The thieves took one really important Louis XV example, an excellent signed *fauteuil*, but left two similar ones. The three together would have been worth five or six times the single. They therefore missed the most important set in the house but carried off half a dozen pleasant middle-nineteenth-century reproductions, which could never be resold for more than £50 each, if that. Clearly they had stolen *au petit bonheur la chance*—picking up objects at random in the hope that they were valuable. In all they took almost fifty separate things; less than ten were valuable, over half were worthless, except for their sentimental value.

How had they broken in? In a very clumsy way which would certainly have led to their capture if the château servants had been even averagely valorous. They drove up in a large van which they parked only about a hundred yards from the house; in the process they passed so close to the outhouses where the servants and gardeners lived, that all the dogs were barking for ten minutes. If they had reconnoitred the house thoroughly in advance they would never have made such a mistake. As it was they were unreasonably lucky. Robert, the *gardien*, woke up but decided on caution.

"There's something going on," he told his wife. "When the dogs stop barking I'll look." He claims he did, and saw nothing, which is hard to believe as the thieves spent at least an hour on the premises.

But they escaped without being disturbed, and the local police investigation hardly posed a threat. They asked questions such as "What were the vases *for*? Did you put flowers in them?" They clearly did not believe the Louis XV chair (which was uninsured) could have been worth £400 at a conservative estimate. The local sergeant left with the words: "I shouldn't worry if I was you, there's lots left."

True, but not much consolation for the Comtesse. None of the stolen items was ever recovered.

In the middle of 1962 André Huré and Claude Mabilotte paid an innocent, afternoon visit to the Château de Ménars, near Bourges, one of the best-known large country houses in France, which now belongs to Colonel Gillard of St. Gobain, the mammoth textile corporation. Ménars contains a varied selection of eighteenth- and nineteenth-century furniture and though they were not able to choose any specific pieces Claude and André knew enough to realise that there must be really valuable—and readily saleable—objects there. They alerted the Richier brothers and, again like ordinary tourists, equipped with cameras and Michelin guides, Xavier and Jean twice made the trip to Ménars, admiring the furniture and taking careful notes. There was yet another preliminary visit. Claude and André returned, after a detailed briefing, and spent an afternoon checking the location of the items that had been specified, and reconnoitring the house and its grounds.

Meanwhile Marcel Bihn in Paris had been inquiring among dealers, finding out who was interested in purchasing a series of eighteenth-century items which he said "had been ordered" and would be available in the near future. Then on the evening of January 15th, 1963, Claude and André set out in their Deux-Chevaux for the final visit to Ménars. On this occasion Claude's canvas sack was in the back though in the end it was not required. Ménars stands less than a mile from a hamlet with four hundred inhabitants but no one noticed the discreet passage of the small Citroën. When they arrived at the main gate Claude got out of the car and was surprised to find the key was in the well-oiled lock. Ménars was wide open, which seemed rather odd. They had become accustomed to raids being easy, but this was absurd. They continued cautiously inside the grounds, arrived at the terrace, and entered by way of the high, glass doors. These too were open and they both realised simultaneously that the house must be occupied.

Claude, who had left his sack on the terrace, was telling André that in the circumstances they would take what they wanted from the grand salon and then get out, without penetrating further into the house, when they were appalled to see all the lights in the room turned on simultaneously. A group of about thirty noisy, joking men flooded in through the main doors, accompanied by two butlers with trays of cocktails. Claude and André were completely ignored—they were both neatly, anonymously dressed—but despite this they both decided to leave as fast as possible. André graciously accepted a drink while Claude tried to look at ease, wondering whether anyone had spotted him dropping his large torch on a Second Empire sofa. It was also disturbing that apart from the butlers they were the only two men in the room without their names displayed on large cards attached to their left lapels. Contrary to their expectations (that the house was only occupied at weekends) Ménars was being used as headquarters for a sales conference of young St. Gobain executives.

Before they had decided which was the least obtrusive exit all the clocks in the salon started to chime seven and the dinner gong sounded. The St. Gobain men had passed a long day studying sales graphs, and within seconds Claude and André were once again alone in the room they had come to rob. If their recent raids had not been so successful they would have headed back to the car with all haste. As it was they had been guaranteed a minimum of £1,500 to do the job, and they decided to trust to their run of luck continuing. They locked all the doors leading from the salon, put the lights out, and started the removals. First a set of transitional Louis XV/XVI *fauteuils* and then a second of Louis XVI chairs in the *médaillon* style, that is with oval backs. There was also the small but rare collection of *potiches de chine*, unusual Chinese porcelain vases which Jean had fancied.

By the time the St. Gobain men had finished their shrimp cocktails the furniture the Richiers had ordered had been removed in two stages, and hidden in a patch of scrub fifty yards from the house. When the two finally arrived at the Place Léon-Blum in the small hours Jean inquired if everything had gone as planned. "It was a very perilous operation," Claude replied suavely. "The auto-route traffic gets more dangerous every day."

CHAPTER VIII

The Police Learn the Trade

Commissaire René Chevalier found that Jacques Dupont's half-facetious remark about the "Gentleman Burglar" had stuck in his mind. He did not talk about it very much—it was too fanciful, and insubstantial, a theory for him to dwell on. And yet it seemed to accord with such facts as he had at his disposal. At first it was a hunch about which he held strong reservations but as time passed it developed into something stronger. Chevalier became almost certain that when, and if, the château gang were finally arrested, their leader would turn out to have more in common with the fictional Arsène Lupin than the real world cat-burglars and house-breakers known to every policeman and catalogued in the Police Judiciaire files. The Commissaire finally decided that traditional methods had become useless. He instructed the G.R.B. not to waste their time chatting to paid informers in dingy bars in the Buttes de Montmartre and solemnly working according to other time-honoured Murder Squad formulae. The large-scale larceny of high quality furniture was, in effect, a new kind of crime, and could only be countered by a new type of policeman. So the Commissaire himself, and his assistants Raton and le Bruchec, went back, rather reluctantly, to school. Their professor was Jacques Dupont.

As personalities, René Chevalier and Dupont might seem hopelessly antipathetic, but the château gang made them complementary. Chevalier is hardly a fashionable figure; his hair is brutally cropped, his bulk would defy the most ingenious tailor, and his taste for acrid rice-paper Gauloises and *pastis* (the anis drink of Marseilles) makes him the exact French counterpart of that cliché of English life, the saloon bar philosopher. There is also another parallel, for externally Chevalier conforms so closely to Maigret, the classic detective of French fiction, that he sometimes seems to be infringing Simenon's copyright. The first time one hears a member of his team respectfully addressing him as "Patron", it looks as though an elaborate parody is being played out. But René Chevalier's speciality is a combination of stolid common sense and an ability to erect a theory on a basis of painstakingly acquired facts, examine it remorselessly, and—if it seems to hold good—push its logical implications to the limit, no matter how unlikely they are. A dedicated pragmatist, Chevalier is also a man without any kind of pretension. He works hard, lives quietly in the suburbs, and when he takes a holiday likes to spend it gardening or fishing. Jacques Dupont is the epitome of Parisian elegance and hyper-sophistication. He was originally trained as a doctor but was temperamentally drawn to the Louvre, where numbers of aesthetes-cum-civil servants are employed on the task of caring for the gigantic collection of objects already owned by the French nation, and of acquiring more. As head of the Historic Monuments department, Dupont's responsibility is for the hundreds of important châteaux throughout France. He works in magnificent offices in the Palais-Royal, only a mile from his apartment overlooking the Place de la Concorde. Walking between the two places, elegant with grey hair and English-cut suit, the ribbon of Commander of the Legion of Honour in his button-hole, he looks what he is—the very model of the top French civil servant. A great attender of aristocratic country weekends, Dupont is always ready to place his expertise at the disposal of the ancient French families—he is frequently called in for advice on some piece of furniture which has come to light, and needs expert identification.

After many conversations with Dupont, Chevalier had built up the equivalent of an Identi-kit portrait of their criminal. He was educated, subtle, and a man with an obsessional interest in the *minutiae* of antiques. There was no question of his concealing it from those who knew him. Perhaps their man was actually an antique dealer. Perhaps he was a raffish aristocrat, who had received training at some stage in his career at the Louvre's admirable school of Beaux Arts, or alternatively at the School of Arts Decoratifs, the "Arts-Déco". (This last hypothesis was highly accurate.) In basic terms, it was impossible that the man behind the château gang was a mere professional criminal who had worked out that eighteenth-century *fauteuils*, mediaeval wooden virgins, or delicate pieces of china had turned into a currency as negotiable as gold sovereigns. This man's knowledge had to be detailed; and he was almost certain to be psychologically abnormal. And so far—Chevalier was forced to accept—he was way ahead of the police, largely because he knew his subject so much better than they did. Accordingly, to get on level terms, the policemen must themselves acquire a certain level of scholarship.

By the end of 1962, René Chevalier and his collaborators, Louis Raton and Joseph le Bruchec, had become familiar figures in the Faubourg St. Honoré. Chevalier spent a lot of time looking in antique dealers' windows, occasionally going inside to pore over an interesting object. At first the dealers took little notice of him—he obviously was not an important collector; his clothes were nothing like elegant enough. They may have thought that he was a dealer himself in a small way, perhaps with a shop somewhere in the provinces, and was simply stopping off to enjoy a tantalising vision of the sort of stock that he himself would never possess. Sometimes he produced a penetrating question; it was clear he knew something about the *haute époque*. In the end he became at least accepted, worthy of a cursory nod, but nothing more. He never actually bought anything and in this rarified atmosphere only the very rich receive anything more than the most perfunctory attention. Chevalier did not qualify as that sort of customer.

About half a mile from Chevalier's office the Faubourg changes to plain rue St. Honoré. Here there are equally glossy dealers, but they are rather more sparse. There are also a few who specialise in selling to the trade. They display their chair-frames un-upholstered, their furniture unpolished and un-restored. (The French taste in general is for antiques with a high gloss on them; so much so that it is often hard to see the wood for the dazzle.) In these few but highly educational shops the Commissaire made the most of his chance to study furniture stripped to the bone. He would spend many mornings poring over the construction of a chair, minutely examining the inlay work on a battered period commode, and very rarely saying anything at all. In these shops, too, he became an accepted figure, his face completely impassive, his spatulate fingers always brushing over the furniture, trying to develop a feel for the crisp edge of fine eighteenth-century carving.

Inside the splendidly restored Palais-Royal, Chevalier began to know his way around the elegant corridors of the Historic Monuments Department. The hushed library with its innumerable scholarly titles was no longer alien; he even came to recognise the code-numbers on the filing cabinets. The connoisseurs' jargon began to make sense, and he realised that their science was as precise as his, their nomenclature as meaningful. Dupont's staff were more helpful than their commercial colleagues in the Faubourg St. Honoré. They good-humouredly tolerated his bewilderment at trying to unravel the academic subtleties of some unusually complicated theft. They lent him reference books, answered his increasingly pointed questions, and guided his team's researches in their world-famous reference library.

A staff of six struggle to keep the catalogue up to date, but it would be a life's work for five times as many. Each time there was a robbery (and by the middle of 1963 thefts seemed to be getting as common as motoring offences) a copy of the local report listing the missing property would be sent to the Historic Monuments Department as well as to the police. The G.R.B.'s job was to examine the *modus operandi* of the crime; the experts in Dupont's office assessed the significance of the stolen objects. Chevalier and Dupont then compared notes and it was not long before they discovered two distinctly similar patterns. In the first place, the methods of entry and exit in virtually every theft of major importance were identical (and very often a small Deux-Chevaux Citroën van was seen in the locality). Secondly, the stolen items all seemed to fall into three very closely defined groups. The thieves specialised in the finest sixteenth- and seventeenth-century ecclesiastical furnishings, usually French tapestries or carved and decorated (polychromed) statues by the most important craftsmen. They were also collecting a rather rare and off-beat ceramic-faïence made in the Marseilles area between about 1720 and 1760. Most significantly, they were also stealing the very best quality eighteenth-century French furniture—but only the products of certain makers. Time and again they had ignored other items which were just as attractive, and sometimes even more saleable. They were only interested in their period. As Dupont astutely pointed out, the pattern of their thefts was an exact parallel of the activity of the most discerning and most commercially successful specialist dealers; those who concentrate on their own chosen periods in antique history, declining even to consider any object not strictly within their speciality, no matter how beautiful (or how great a bargain) the occasional find might appear to be. Dupont was fascinated by the academic knowledge behind the thefts, and also by the highly-developed commercial acumen. He was beginning to understand the taste. These people were stealing items today which he, and a handful of other specialists, would have predicted as the latest vogue in the Salle Drouot, the Paris equivalent of Christie's or Sotheby's, a year hence. In Dupont's view it was not just a question of scholarship; their man, wherever he might be, knew all about the French royal cabinet-makers, but he was also extraordinarily sensitive to the apparently unpredictable shifts in fashion which characterise the most sophisticated end of the antique trade. He seemed to combine these rare gifts with the flair for anticipating price levels which is found in all the really successful figures of the antique-dealing fraternity.

Chevalier realised that his information about the personality of the thief would have to be drawn from a very detailed examination of the thefts themselves. Accordingly he and his assistants in the G.R.B. decided to embark on another, even more thorough analysis of the third and largest group of thefts—those of fine Louis XIV and Louis XV furniture. The Faubourg St. Honoré policemen approached their subject like aspiring art historians. They began a careful study of late seventeenth-century and *haute époque* furniture to discover what it was really like. They discovered a vision of luxuriance, and found that the elements that went to construct furniture of this quality were like an inventory of Ali Baba's cave. The finest, most elaborately matched woods combined with bronze, gold and silver leaf, and tapestry. To heighten the effect there was porcelain, ebony, inlays of pewter, brass, silver, and tortoise-shell. Marble and precious stones of all kinds added their individual lustre. And the whole extraordinary output was controlled and regulated by a central administration, working by a set of rules of unrivalled intricacy, and also solemnity. There was a strong contrast between the earnestness of the process and the comparative frivolity of its end product. The effort—and the expense—was the French eighteenth-century equivalent of the Russian moon programme. The sums that the Bourbon monarchs of this age were prepared to spend on furniture are breathtaking. For example, the Grand Bureau of Louis XV (described as *à cylindre*—that is, the original roll-top desk) cost £2,515 in 1768, or at least £30,000 in present-day terms. The commode Louis XVI ordered from Jean-Henri Riesener on his accession cost £1,014 (about £12,000 today). In this situation, the craftsmen, as snobbish and petulant as present-day *couturiers*, often became so indispensable that they could afford to dictate the taste of their aristocratic clients. Cohorts of bureaucrats documented virtually every item produced by the leading cabinet-makers; one incidental result of this is that modern experts, by searching through the bulging archives, can assess and sometimes even identify apparently quite obscure pieces of *haute époque* furniture.

In 1663 Louis XIV and his minister Colbert devoted an extraordinary amount of energy to ensuring that all royal furniture was catalogued individually, cross-referenced with bills of sale, records of subsequent disposal, and meticulous descriptions of repairs or adaptation. For 130 years this practice continued and the records have survived, eighteen huge volumes detailing the beauties and sometimes lunacies of French classical furniture. This *Journal du Garde Meuble* is available for inspection to anyone. The conscientious entries are a monumental tribute to the Bourbons' passion for magnificence and also, for the unscrupulous scholar prepared to delve deeply enough, a positive invitation to dishonesty. As a leading authority on the *haute époque* has said: "In one way the records are a kind of licence for larceny."

CHAPTER IX

How They Destroyed Versailles

Xavier Richier had for some years numbered the dusty volumes of the *Journal du Garde Meuble* among his favourite books. Unfortunately the journal comes to an end in 1792, where there is a gap until the 1870s when similar attempts at cataloguing, on a less ambitious scale, appear once more in the archives. Comparatively few aristocrats went to the guillotine in the first of the modern revolutions; it could be argued that the heaviest aristocratic casualties of all were counted among the furniture which the Bourbon monarchs and their satellites had been amassing over the previous century and a half.

The royal furniture, an extraordinary testament to the Bourbons' determination to create, whatever the expense, the golden age of decorative art, became a symbol for the revolutionaries in the same way as the palaces themselves. After the royal family had been imprisoned in 1792 Robespierre did his best to ensure that these enormous, arrogant houses would never again be fit for occupation by any future aristocratic tyrant. He also had more pressing problems—how to provide food, and how to reconstitute the mismanaged and depleted army and navy. Foreign suppliers required payment in something harder than the promissory notes which the French had recently been obliged to issue. Therefore, on June 10th, 1793, with these priorities in mind apart from any ideological considerations, the Revolutionary Convention passed the "Law relating to the Sale

of the Furniture of the Garde Meuble Nationale, and the Former Civil List". Its preamble proclaimed that the Convention
was passing the law to "put to the service of the defence of
liberty . . . the sumptuous furniture of the last tyrants of
France." And so, in a blaze of revolutionary purple prose, began
the dispersal of almost all the royal furniture, ardently abetted
by British, American and Greek entrepreneurs. When the Convention decided to turn furniture into cash, there was no short-
age of buyers. In the last hundred years crafty antique dealers
have devised many ingenious methods of exploiting the ignorant. The revolutionary sales, which lasted more or less contin-
uously from August 25th, 1793, until October 19th, 1795, were
the most dishonest ever. The story would fill the heart of every
such dealer with an exquisite nostalgia for a golden age that
can never come again. A kind of running report on the sales
was made at the time by the Baron Davillier and these are still
available in the archives of the department of the Seine-et-Oise

The Revolutionary Convention appointed a group of commissioners, the *Commissaires-Priseurs*, to value the confiscated
furniture and supervise its disposal. Unfortunately for the revolutionary exchequer some of the most disreputable dealers in
Paris succeeded in getting into the game. They began by pro-
curing a law exempting the royal pieces from export duty; combined to undervalue the furniture grotesquely; sold it to themselves at absurd prices; and finally resold it, mostly abroad, at
profit margins which sometimes attained several thousand per
cent. This system only applied to one category of items—valued
at under £1,000—the modern currency equivalent would be
£15,000. The furniture in this category was for sale immediately
to anyone prepared to pay the (rigged) valuation. The Convention had decreed that the other objects valued at more than
£1,000 should be sold after appropriate cataloguing and adver-
tisement by public auction—the bidding to last for the duration
of an inch of candle, that is the purchaser would be the man
with the highest bid standing when the candle was snuffed.

The second system provided marginally greater difficulties
for the dishonest dealers, but they resolved them by devising
a formula that has become the basis of rigged sales since. Despite
periodic complaints from private individuals distressed that

77

their goods have fetched perhaps one tenth of their true value, it shows no sign of abating. The Paris dealers formed a "Ring", with its own complex etiquette, much of which has been passed down intact to contemporary practice. At the public sale the members of the Ring agree not to bid against each other, thus keeping the prices artificially low. After the sale, they hold their private auction, buying what they want, and paying the poorer members of the Ring a commission for not having bid before and thereby inflating the prices. The operation of a Ring can often be detected by a private individual at a sale, but he seldom has either the knowledge or the capital to do anything about it. This happened to the Abbé Gregoire, a priest with an interest in furniture, and he wrote an impassioned memorandum complaining to the Revolutionary Convention. It is an acute piece of polemic, and provides a graphic account of what went on. "I have watched the so-called commissioners in action," the indignant Abbé wrote. "When they fear the honesty of educated people, amateurs or craftsmen, they offer them money to withdraw from the sale. They agree among themselves not to bid, in order to keep the prices low, and in at least one place have grievously assaulted a bidder who was raising the prices to something approaching the furniture's true value." Despite his gift for outraged prose, the priest failed to get anything done about it. The commissioners sold most of the furniture in the American, German, and British markets, and also, to quote a contemporary record, "to certain Greek captains". The most important purchaser was James Swan, a Boston banker, who thus has a claim to being the founder of a tradition which has more or less held good ever since—that the finest products of European culture are exported to the New World, often well below their proper value. The revolutionary government was effectively cheated by its own commissioners but it managed to offset the effect of this at least to some extent by running another major swindle. Government officials discreetly approached a number of important foreign buyers, again mainly Americans, Greeks and members of the English nobility, inviting them to come to Paris and buy important pieces direct. There was only one problem. Very early on the new rulers realised that a piece of furniture from Fontainebleau or the Trianon fetched a better price than a similar piece from one of the minor residences, offices or warehouses attached to the royal household. They were also astute enough to see that it was not entirely a question of quality; the appeal of a piece actually originating "from Versailles" was enormous, particularly in America. And after eighteen months of intensive disposal even that vast treasure-house of furniture was beginning to run low. The revolutionary government took the obvious course, and guaranteed the provenance of crate-loads of objects as being from one royal palace or another. If the buyer still had any doubts, they were also perfectly ready to authenticate an individual piece as the personal property of Marie-Antoinette or Louis XIV, and, if necessary, of both.

Such pieces found a ready market among the new capitalist rich in America, many going to plantation owners in the south. Few if any of the items were genuine, but they provided a pool of furniture which became the basis of the fantastic, somewhat unreal price structure which has prevailed in the American market ever since. Fortunately for the French national heritage there was a tendency among the more perceptive public officials to grab the better pieces to furnish their own offices. Much furniture in this category eventually returned to the government and is now in the Louvre or in the reconstituted sections of Versailles. Many other pieces found their way to the newly acquired estates of the commercial bourgeoisie, where they stayed anonymously until time had made them respectable again. Many of the most magnificent pieces went to England and the Prince Potocki purchased twenty coachloads to furnish his Polish estates. One item he bought was a copy of the famous *Bureau du Roi*, stamped by Riesener; it found its way back to France clandestinely in 1948, and is now in a villa near Cassis on the French south coast. But for about eighty years, most of the furniture vanished from sight altogether. Many of the new owners felt inhibited because the furniture had been stolen; taste changed under the influence of the Emperor Napoleon, and it became in any case no longer fashionable. Pieces that had been used in government offices were stripped of their "royal" embellishments; fleur-de-lys and royal cyphers were replaced by porcelain plaques, thousands of gold and silver ornaments, bronze lamp brackets, and candle-sticks were melted down. The palace ledgers, which still survive, frequently have entries over-written with the curt note: "To the Mint."

From Xavier Richier's point of view the historical fate of the royal furniture was highly interesting. It meant that the felonious scholar, patiently examining the contents of one great house or another, might occasionally come across something from one of the great palaces. Clearly pieces of this calibre could not be sold undisguised on the open market, even if their rightful owners were so ignorant about their possessions that they would not have identified them. But Richier naturally did not care about this, unlike Marcel Bihn and Claude Mabilotte. For some time he had made a practice of stealing selected items without any question of resale; he did not despise money—far from it—but his personal collection always came first.

From the end of the nineteenth century a small group of scholars, researchers and civil servants have been at work in succession to try and bring the dispersed *haute époque* furniture back again, to restore the Bourbon palaces, and to make sure that great furniture was not left to rot in obscure places. Jacques Dupont now carries on this tradition; for twenty years he has been searching out *haute époque* furniture in the interest of the French nation. The restoration of a small but unique château in northern Burgundy, which was begun in 1960, was perhaps his most cherished scheme. He set out to recreate a setting as near as possible identical to one which had existed in the 1650s. He succeeded quite remarkably by any standards, and ironically, in this way he provided the ultimate technical challenge to Xavier Richier. The château is located close to the village of Montbard. Its name is Bussy-Rabutin.

CHAPTER X

The Raid on Bussy-Rabutin

The château stands about five miles from the Burgundian village of Montbard, neatly tucked into a bend of the wooded hills that border the road running south to Avallon. It is moated, and fully fortified, but not even the most optimistic military men could claim that it was sited strategically. The château looks like a hideaway, not a strong-point, a place for assignations, not battles. This is hardly surprising, for though Bussy-Rabutin, or Bussy-le-Grand as it used to be called, was built by a man famous for his swordsmanship, his memory as a historical figure is due to his achievements as one of the most consistent libertines produced by an age and class dedicated to promiscuity.

Le Chevalier Roger de Rabutin, Comte du Bussy, was born at Epiry on April 13th, 1618, and had acquired his first mistress while still attending the Jesuit school at Autun. At sixteen he accompanied his father to war—to the siege of Lorraine, and there resolved to become a professional soldier. Basically a mercenary, he served under numerous flags, and claimed to know all the leading military commanders in Europe. His speciality was siege warfare, and in the long static months outside the walls of towns ranging from Stockholm to Naples, he built up a reputation as a swordsman of the highest class, an inveterate duellist and an unscrupulous rake, with a growing trail of illegitimate children across seven countries. He had quickly discovered that his prowess with rapier or a pair of pistols was such that there were few husbands or fathers who dared to intervene. Bussy tended to pick his quarrels with people well-connected at court, and this, coupled with his great gifts for seduction, resulted in his constantly incurring the displeasure of either the King, the Church, his employers, or all three. On two occasions he was thrown into jail; countless times he was banished from Court to his country estate near Montbard for a month or so, until mourning was over for his late opponent, or the lady had been married off, despatched to a nunnery, or had acquired another lover. Bussy spent these "exiles" decorating his house. He literally painted it—the walls are covered with portraits of his friends and relations, acquaintances and mistresses, generals and Dukes, foreign commanders, allies and enemies. And, because he was a conceited man, the portraits of a great many ladies, delicately explained by the authorities to be his relatives, and known by the locals, to whom he is still something of a hero, as the "Gallery of Virgins". Bussy was also a gifted writer. During a busy life, he found time to produce a readable autobiography, and a highly repetitive catalogue of his campaigns in the bedrooms of Europe called *Histoire Amoureuse des Gaules*. Here, he describes with relish and occasional unexpected coyness his experiences ranging from a curious affair with a hermaphrodite, to the more scandalous debaucheries at Court. Just as his serious work secured his election to the *Académie Française* in 1665, his foray into literary titillation was secretly published. The ensuing scandal nearly cost him his head, and he was thrown into the Bastille. Released eventually by Louis XIV, he was given a pension, but banned from Paris. Whatever his demerits, Bussy possessed style, and it is recorded that when challenged to fight a duel by night, he replied: "Bussy is not wont to display his valour to the stars, nor even to the moon, since they are unable to contemplate him properly, or appreciate his skill." He got his way, and fought the duel in the morning, killing both challenger and second within ten minutes. He at last died of apoplexy shortly after learning his daughter had been seduced. So ended an inspiring biography.

This then was the man whose home and extraordinary personality, both nearly forgotten, now excited the imagination of Jacques Dupont. When the state took over the château, it was

furnished much as it had been at the beginning of the eighteenth
century. Although many pieces of the decorations were missing,
the stonework was crumbling, the tapestries moth-eaten, the roof
leaking like a sieve, most important from Dupont's point of
view, the château and its contents were exceptionally well documented. The bills and receipts for much of its construction were
neatly filed away, and Bussy's old inventories, the testament of
a military and thoroughly well-ordered mind, provided the
department with a solid base to start their task of reconstruc-
tion. It was simply a question of dedicated research among the
documents preserved by the Ministry. The château became a
favourite of the department's staff, and those concerned were
only too pleased to get out of Paris and routine work by slipping
down to Montbard, taking the village bus to the eight kilometre
stone on the Dijon road, and then walking for the last part of
the journey up the little valley, which is as tranquil as in Bussy's
time. Woods surround the château on three sides, the fourth is
open to the narrow side-road, empty except for the passing farm
cart, and bordered by a plain stone wall. The gates are simple,
and a short curving drive passes the lodge where the custodian
lives, crosses the moat by way of a small fixed bridge, and then
reaches the building itself. In common with most buildings of
its period, the main door is on the north side, facing a broad
yard, which is flanked by stables and servants' quarters. The
hall gives on to a curving staircase, set in the massive stone
walls, which leads up to the main reception rooms. Here great
windows facing south open on to a balcony which has its own
stairs leading to the formal Italianate garden. There are two
salons, a retiring room (for ladies), and a small but lavishly
decorated bedroom. The rooms are lined with portraits, the ceil-
ings decorated with pastoral scenes, the beams painted and
carved. If the paintings were less personal and evocative of their
original owner the effect would be overpowering. As it is, the
overall impression is successful, though all the rules of decoration are broken. Muted, sometimes faded, colours blend with
the wood block floors, the warm stone of the window lintels, and
the agreeable, unpretentious furniture. Bussy was a well-connected courtier but still a long way from the top of the contemporary hierarchy. Versailles protocol forbade anyone of his rank

to indulge in too much ostentation; the quality of a man's furniture, as well as virtually every other detail of his life, had to obey fixed rules.

The most sumptuous furniture was the prerogative of the King alone; even his children and the Dukes of the royal blood had to take care that their tastes did not overlap his. If the King chose gold leaf then his children had to content themselves with silver. Several degrees lower down, the courtiers were restricted to painted furniture, only occasional high points being embossed. Such subtleties of status, which would have provided hilarious material for a contemporary sociologist, had such a category been thought of, occupied much time and passion. Discussions about which *ébéniste* should receive the commission to design the Queen's new dressing-table often assumed major proportions.

Even Bussy, to his chagrin, far from Versailles, was governed by the rules of the Court. His furniture, therefore, was comparatively plain. A broad, stoutly-made bed, a commode of drawers by a local craftsman, a heavy cupboard for clothes, some walnut side-tables. But there were a few grander items; a pair of console tables, for instance, their tops fashioned in scagliola marble, and his collection of chairs, which revealed that he was a man who knew the sophisticated taste of the capital.

Both salons contained sets of chairs, lining the walls with the rigid regimentation of the Court. They must have been Bussy's pride because they were all the work of Boulard, a full set of at least twenty-four chairs, and probably a pair of sofas as well. Most of these had disappeared by the time the Historic Monuments Department took over Bussy-le-Grand; only four chairs and one sofa had survived. Their frames were in perfect order; they all bore Boulard's *estampille*, or signature, but the tapestry covering them was torn and, inevitably, badly faded. Dupont set about refurnishing the two salons as authentically as possible, which was a major work. From dossiers in the Louvre he isolated and acquired, over several years, twenty contemporary copies of Bussy's chairs. They were made of the same wood (walnut); they were of identical age to within a few years; they may even have been built from the same template as the originals, although they lacked the master craftsman's signature. When his set was complete Dupont had all the chairs covered in contemporary seat tapestry, which was nailed over the seats and therefore completely obscured Boulard's signature on the four originals. Short of removing the tapestry again it was virtually impossible to say which chairs were original and which were contemporary copies.

Dupont and his staff were content with their work. When one of the French glossy magazines wished to produce an illustrated feature on the restorations they were flattered and pleased to cooperate. The article concentrated mainly on the portrait gallery and the Italian garden but mentioned in passing that the chairs were an unusual mixture by Boulard and contemporary copyists. One of the magazine's most devoted subscribers, Xavier Richier, put a double cross in the margin beside this reference. After that it was only a matter of time.

Easter 1963 was unusually hot in Burgundy, and the Sunday before there was a minor heat-wave. The morning train from Paris produced four passengers, whom the station-master vaguely recalled afterwards: three men and a woman. Most of the population were either at Mass or still in bed and it was too early for the regular patrons of the Station Hotel, Montbard's one claim to distinction. The Paris passengers made straight for it, ordered drinks and an elaborate meal, and settled down to wait. They had made a study of Montbard before arriving and therefore must have known that a major gastronomic experience awaited them.

Monsieur Albert Belin, proprietor of the Station, holds the title of Maître Chef de France. He is now in semi-retirement and is content with two Michelin stars, which means his restaurant is as good, if not better, than any in New York or London, and that there are perhaps four better thought of restaurants in Paris (all of them more than three times as expensive). M. Belin takes his art seriously and Sunday luncheon, eaten beneath an array of certificates testifying to complex culinary distinctions, is a familial but not a convivial occasion. Patrons appear in quiet groups after late Mass, study the four-page menu as if it were a thesis (which practically it is) and submerge themselves in food served by solid, knowledgeable waitresses. A typical menu, the recommended house specialities, consists of *Escargots de Bourgogne*, with a whiff of nutmeg; *Truito Farcie*, with Chablis; and the famous *Saulpicquet Montbardois*, Belin's most famous dish—ham rolls stuffed with asparagus, spiced cherries dusted with cinnamon, and *périgord* sauce. The chef advises Romasnee Contee, 1927, as a complement, one of 300 vintages in his cellars.

The strangers, who made more noise than the regulars, left at two-thirty to catch the yellow bus which spasmodically connects Montbard to Dijon. By an odd bureaucratic quirk the morning bus departs from the square at eleven-forty precisely, which means that it can usually be seen from the arriving Paris train, but has invariably pulled away before even the most swift-footed traveller can race through the station to catch it. This system is inconvenient, except for M. Belin, but Paris-Montbard is an unusual itinerary.

The afternoon bus left at two-forty, on time, and twenty minutes later after a bumpy ride the strangers were walking up the incline that leads to Bussy-le-Grand. Henri, the château's *gardien*, was surprised and annoyed to hear their steps on the gravel. He was officially on duty, but the château had only just been opened to the public and he had not expected any visitors before Easter. He had eaten a solid lunch, and had decided to take a siesta. He pulled on his trousers and hurried down from his temporary set of slightly primitive rooms in the servants' quarters in the château's remote east wing, overlooking the moat. (The *gardien*'s rooms have since been changed to a superior apartment in the gate-house which is also better strategically from the point of view of checking on intruders. In those days neither he nor the authorities were much concerned about this aspect of his duties.)

Henri, a retired soldier with a red nose, consoled himself with the thought of a forthcoming tip, and launched into the conducted tour—he had been supplied with a script by the Historic Monuments Department but had not so far memorised it very well. It was not long before he decided that he did not like his first visitors, and indeed they caused him certain misgivings about his new job, which had previously seemed ideal. As a newcomer to the profession Henri had assumed that a conducted tour meant what it said—he would march the grateful tourists round in a disciplined manner, recite his Historic Monuments patter, and occasionally answer a meek question. But it did not work out like this. The two smaller men "pranced"—this was Henri's picturesque word—all over the house, opening the large windows, sprinting round the garden, and tossing pebbles in the moat. One moment they were at the bottom of the garden, the next on the second floor. And while they dashed about the big man, later described by Henri as "a huge, bronzed type, like a circus strong-man", stayed with the woman in the main salon, apparently more interested in taking photographs than anything the guide had to say. Henri was torn between his inbred authoritarian instincts, his desire for a tip, and the uneasy feeling that somehow they were making a fool of him.

"The big fellow and the girl behaved," he later told the police. "They looked like newly-weds. But the other men were very peculiar . . ." At this point he probably made that gesture, a tug at the ear with the thumb and index finger of the left hand, which indicates homosexuality the length of the littoral from Barcelona to Naples. But Henri failed to express himself clearly enough for the official mind.

He was probably still confused. After a few minutes his patience had cracked and pinning down the two undisciplined visitors he explained that they were supposed to follow him, not rampage about. They all returned to the salon where the big man, who was carrying enough lenses for the most exacting professional as well as two cameras and a tripod, had moved several chairs "because the light is bad". Henri began to complain when the woman asked him for a glass of water, very politely, and he marched off reluctantly to his kitchen, thinking again of his tip. When he returned he found they were photographing the under sides of the chairs, which was too much for him. He assumed they were all mad.

The visitors examined every object in the place with deep interest and stayed until nearly five, when they left to catch the bus back. By then they had mollified Henri slightly by asking questions about his job and his living quarters and insisting on taking his photograph. Unfortunately when they did leave, satisfied they had learnt everything they needed, the big man

had the insolence to offer their guide one new franc (roughly
1s. 10d.) as a tip. Henri returned belatedly to bed with the dis-
agreeable feeling that he had been duped, which was correct,
although he was yet to learn in precisely what way. The visitors
had only completed half their job; they would be back again,
causing further upsets and disruption.

Henri never received his photograph but one morning soon
after the strange visit he walked heavily into the salon, stopped
dead, and peered vaguely round. It was all somehow . . . bare.
He started to count deliberately, and recount . . .

When Jacques Dupont was told that the four signed Boulards
had been stolen, and these four only, he was flatly incredulous.
And the thieves, he asked the police, no clues? Nothing. "So
they came like fairies in the night," Dupont said sarcastically.
The highly correct Historic Monuments chief was naturally un-
aware of the double meaning.

CHAPTER XI

The Decorators

If Henri had been more knowing about social life in his country's capital he could have saved both Commissaire Chevalier and Jacques Dupont a great deal of inconvenience. But he was a poor witness when it came to detail. The Dijon police spent a lot of time interviewing him without extracting the one fact that might have given Chevalier the break-through his investigation so badly needed. Henri repeated time and again that the Bussy-le-Grand visitors had been "peculiar" and "odd", but the police from Dijon did not understand that he was trying to say "homosexual". Given this information Chevalier would certainly have started to think in terms of Paris homosexual circles and, by extension, the numerous specialists in Camp. He knew about Camp decorators but had never thought to connect their taste with that of the château thieves, because the two were so dissimilar.

A basic element of Camp is that it should be immediately recognisable to other devotees, but incomprehensible to non-initiates. It provides a way of publicly expressing the will to shock and irritate. The impulse and its expression are not far from those that were current among the thousand or so nobles at the Court of Louis XV at Versailles, leading them to develop special uniforms, their own accent, and a coterie vocabulary to ensure that their difference from the *haute bourgeoisie* would never be blurred. This passion became all the more burning as the bourgeois grew as rich, and sometimes even richer, than their social superiors imprisoned in the perpetual aristocratic weekend of Versailles, Fontainebleau or Marly. The bourgeois could amass fortunes through business: the *noblesse* only had at their disposal the means of getting rid of money. Their eccentricities were taken to such lengths that a lady of the Court could immediately be told from a member of the grand bourgeois families simply by the way she walked. (The approved Versailles gait seems to have been a short-stepped, breathless shuffle; the reverse, paradoxically, of stately elegance. Not that this mattered: the point, of course, was that they walked *differently*, not better.)

Twentieth-century Camp is usually associated with homosexuality, though there are many Paris dealers specialising in Camp articles who are as heterosexual as Adam. Both Jean Richier and André Huré were homosexual and had never made any attempt to hide it. In the case of Huré, rather the reverse. Marcel Bihn could not have been more masculine. Mabilotte was basically heterosexual but after a long apprenticeship on the Camp fringe of the Paris antique trade had picked up a good many of its mannerisms. Jean and Huré were the embodiment of Decorators' Camp both in their taste and their personalities. For years they had specialised in curiosities and fashionable trifles—junk, but junk which was trendy and relatively profitable. Their finds were the kind that could be used to decorate a small restaurant "amusingly": *"amusant"* is the key word in the Camp decorator's vocabulary.

Jean was particularly well equipped for this trade. He moved with the fashions, and often ahead of them. In the middle 1950s, fresh out of the School of Decorative Arts, he was purchasing *amusant* Victoriana, which later increased in value enormously. He switched rapidly to *Art Nouveau*, the so-called *Style du Métro* of the 1890s which had recently enjoyed a vogue, and a consequent increase in price. When *Art Nouveau* grew scarce he switched again, this time to objects made in the 1920s, particularly lamps, ash-trays, and those curious gramophones decorated with "electronic" flashes, their design influenced by jazz-age verticism. Nothing could be more remote from the *haute époque* furniture which the château robbers stole. The police concentrated on the "classical" section of the Paris trade in their search for outlets, certain that some really valuable items were being sold, one way or another, through legitimate channels. In his investigations René Chevalier had ignored the Camp end of the trade altogether.

It was too cheap, the taste involved was too different from the taste he had already deduced. Camp provided a perfect camouflage; almost as good as that of a country doctor. Jean and his shadow Claude were accepted figures in the half-dozen or so main centres where the Paris antiques trade flourishes, but were always on the fringe. They would never buy or sell objects costing more than a maximum of £100, and they were mainly interested in eccentricities of one kind and another—things like Victorian dolls, particularly the wooden ones with articulated limbs, which became collectors' items in the early 1960s, especially when their wigs were refurbished, their faces rouged and provided with long, false eyelashes. At the same time it was essential that the bodies of the dolls should not be renovated at all; the more battered the better. Jean was also something of a specialist in so-called "English" military chests, their corners capped with brass, their drawers fitted with (contemporary) recessed handles, a long way after the style which was popular at the very end of the eighteenth century and in the English Regency period. Made of oldish mahogany, usually from Victorian wardrobes, these could be skilfully embellished, perhaps with a brass plate saying they belonged to an "officer during the Napoleonic wars". They sold well and were often used as cocktail or china cabinets. To complete his bizarre stock-in-trade, Jean also specialised in hands: the small wooden lasts used by Victorian glove-makers. He sold these to boutiques where they were displayed as chi-chi presents.

During his daily trips along the most important concentration of antique shops in Paris, the rue St. Honoré, René Chevalier came across the occasional shop dealing in Camp. He paid them little attention because he knew that they never had genuine antiques (dating before 1830) on the premises, let alone a commode by Riesener or a set of signed Boulard chairs of the kind that were disappearing. At the intersection of the rue Royale, the rue St. Honoré turns into the rue du Faubourg St.

Honoré, and the two form a sinuous corridor of elegance a mile long, the Paris equivalent of Fifth Avenue or Bond Street. It is an area containing the finest connoisseurs, and some of the most shameless swindlers in a trade which specialises in them. The elaborately decorated windows display exquisite pieces and impudent fakes in equal proportions—many with their price tags marked in dollars, revealing the dealers' widely-shared prejudice that Americans are bigger suckers than native-born Frenchmen, which is doubtful judging by the prices rich Parisians are prepared to pay in the interest of *chic*. One shop, where René Chevalier finally succeeded towards the end of the hunt in recovering an important *fauteuil* (stolen from the Château de Corbeville which belongs to Genevieve Fath, widow of the couturier), has a close-circuit television lens poking its camouflaged nose through the curlicues of a fine Louis XV mirror in the long entrance hall. This ensures that assistants upstairs can keep an eye on stray clients below, and provides, incidentally, an excellent symbol of the Paris antiques trade. This shop's stock is typically eclectic; there are a few genuine items, some of very high quality. There are also examples of very modern manufacture indeed; some so new that anyone with experience can see at once that they are only a matter of months old. They display at the front of the shop, as a kind of speciality of the house, a pair of wood and plaster statues of negroes known as "Blackamoors", usually holding bowls or trays. The style grew up in Venice in the eighteenth century. Such figures often stood at the main entrances of *palazzi* on the canals, and visitors, apart from being enchanted by the expertise of the carver Viani, the best known Venetian craftsman who produced Blackamoors, used the trays for leaving their visiting cards. The style is often highly sensual, sometimes erotic; there is always a man and a woman, the female body rounded and undulating, the male face that of a boy, usually wearing an expression of supplication and misery. A pair of the statues appeal to a broad spectrum of sexual taste but as a decoration they tend to be overpowering in any environment less rococo than a Venetian palace. They are extremely fashionable in the Camp circles of Paris.

Any knowing collector would realise that the chances of finding a pair of genuine Blackamoors of the eighteenth century is very remote; Viani's own output was limited; it took several decades for the style to catch on outside Venice, and it was only at the beginning of the nineteenth century that copies were produced in any number—and these were invariably poor pastiches of Viani's work, done in such a perfunctory way that fakes do not require a very practised eye to detect. A genuine pair would probably fetch between three and five thousand dollars at a good sale—not a huge price, but Blackamoors are not the kind of item that most connoisseurs get very excited about. In this shop the statues, always new-looking and shiny, cost $5,000, an excellent price for a genuine pair.

For nearly ten years Jean had dealt in similar rubbish, but by 1962 he was a decorator with a head start over his colleagues. He had access, unlike them, to a truly astonishing range of furniture and objects. The safest way to dispose of stolen pieces was to place them directly with a private client rather than to sell them through the trade (there was always a risk that while on public show their original owner or an agent might recognise them). So Jean concentrated his energies on building up his clientèle and expanding his reputation as a decorator, and one who had a flair for acquiring good furniture, quickly and at a reasonable price. He was highly successful but there were still not enough clients to buy all the furniture he had. It was not surprising; the syndicate's supply was virtually unlimited. They were, after all, using the churches and châteaux of the Ile de France as their stock-room.

CHAPTER XII

The Great Year

For Jean the situation was ideal, and he rapidly acquired a new *persona* to match his success. He adopted the airs of a prosperous decorator; the *gamin* look, the carefree, childish personality, these had gone for ever. He also developed some of his brother's superciliousness. He treated his clients as philistines (rather like Xavier treated Mabilotte and Huré) and revealed unsuspected gifts as a salesman. His approach to a commission he received in Christmas 1962 (the decoration of an elegant apartment in the rue de Longchamp) was typical of the new Jean. In the visits he succeeded in brainwashing his client, convincing him that he "absolutely *must*" furnish his new home with *haute époque* furniture, and that only the genuine objects would do. Jean emphasised the magnificent (and prestigious) décor this kind of furniture would create; by chance he knew where he could get hold of precisely what was required—and at the knockdown price of £3,500. Jean's final argument, that genuine antiques were in any case the best possible investment, clinched the matter.

But there was one snag; Jean had been lying. He had no idea where to get the objects he needed. Naturally, he consulted Xavier, who checked his research dossier and suggested a number of "possibles", including the Château de Ménars, near Bourges. The brothers reconnoitred; it was okay. Jean offered

André and Claude (who had spotted Ménars originally) £1,500 to get what he wanted.

As Jean's order was for considerably less than they could conveniently manage in two trips, they in turn consulted Xavier and then Marcel—who provided detailed instructions on what else to select. His list included a fine set of signed Louis XVI chairs, *style médaillon*—with oval backs. In January, André and Claude accomplished the robbery with even more insolence than usual, under the eyes of the St. Gobain salesmen. Jean took his six chairs, and Claude and André gave him a set of fine Chinese porcelain vases (*potiches de Chine*) as a gesture of goodwill. The conveyor-belt operation proceeded with the efficiency it had acquired since Bihn's arrival. Jean delivered the four transitional chairs, unmodified, to his delighted client. He gave the other two to Xavier, as his percentage, and disposed of the vases privately, one of them going as a present to his personal doctor. Meanwhile, Marcel and Claude took the six *médaillons* to Gonzales-Sotto in the rue de Charonne the next morning; they had warned him a fortnight earlier to leave himself free for a rush job.

The restorer, and Massé, his *tapissier*, worked precisely to Marcel's specifications. In ten days, they had altered the feet, made the seats into *"bois naturel"* instead of gilt, and modified the *estampilles*, the original craftsman's signature, for good measure. Marcel—with his usual foresight—had alerted one of the *doyens* of Paris antiques, Maître Solomon Blache, to the news that they had some particularly good *médaillons* in mind for him. As he said (in the language of the trade): "You'll go for them. They have your signature all over them."

Blache duly bought them for nearly £3,000, in good faith, and resold them at a fair profit. Marcel, Claude and André split the proceeds equally, deducting the rue de Charonne bill of £150 from the total. Claude and André split Jean's cash and also the receipts from the sale of small individual *objets d'art* they had removed, again on Xavier's advice, to ballast their load. They ended up with £3,000 each for an evening's work, and gave Xavier a gift of candlesticks. The same system was used for a raid on the Château de la Bouleaunière in April, and Villarceaux, the Duc de Villefranche's house, in August. As far as technique goes, they had reached their peak. For the gang, the summer of 1963 was when the going was good.

All of them made trips to North Africa with Marcel at different times—he had a small orange-farm in Tunisia. André nearly finished paying for his apartment in the rue Dauphine (originally he had borrowed the down-payment from an old friend "Bruno" Bunau-Varilla, who now got his loan back). André blossomed into a kind of Camp peacock, and played up to the jocular reputation for sartorial splendour he had acquired among the dealers at the Hotel Rameau, the Versailles version of the Hotel Drouot, where he went regularly. Nowadays his elaborate silk pleated shirts, made to measure, bore the label of Sulka in the Place Vendôme. Claude, whose sex life had improved with his finances, embarked on a series of extrovert *affaires*. He was now totally separated from his wife, Monique Carin, whom he had married in May, 1956. They remained on friendly terms, and he provided for her and their daughter generously; but knowing Claude of old, Monique cannily went on working, part-time, as a telephone operator. Jean was planning to open an exclusive shop with Xavier and his mother. They also talked about buying a grand new apartment in the Marais not far from the Louvre; Jean was interested in the magnificent Place des Vosges, where Victor Hugo had lived.

All the syndicate looked back on the summer of 1963 with an almost Proustian nostalgia: Africa, afternoons drinking in the shop on Quai Malaquais, weekends in Liévin. Here the atmosphere was both gay and familial; Madame Richier and a girl-friend of Marcel's or Claude's would descend on the local supermarket to give Xavier a break from the unsurpassable awfulness of the food cooked by his maid, Solange. Everyone would visit churches or châteaux (as respectable tourists). They specialised in obscene queer jokes in front of the Curé Bernaud, who was both scandalised and titillated. And Marcel introduced an element of muscular boisterousness which, as an unwelcome variant on Xavier's habitual eccentricities and total indifference to his neighbours, made the "mad menagerie" at six bis, rue Theirs, more unpopular than ever with the Liévin neighbours.

The climax, which the gang remembered with delight, came on a typically sepulchral Liévin Sunday afternoon. Marcel, stripped to the waist, and Jean, shrieking like a madman, were riding a horse in Xavier's chaotic garden. When the animal showed signs of sexual restlessness, their yells, encouraging the others to come and admire the scene, could be heard half a mile away. Finally, they horrified the woman next door by urinating in the garden—until Madame Richier shouted hoarse reprimands from upstairs.

It couldn't last. There were already one or two clouds in their Indian Summer, notably Xavier's supercilious crankiness, and a general irritation at the disparity between the true value of the objects they stole (when disposed of with publicity and well-authenticated pedigrees) and the prices they actually achieved, even with Marcel's good management and experience. Their total haul for the first half of 1963, if it had been sold by the legal owners at Sotheby's or Christie's in London, or on Fifth Avenue, would probably have fetched nearly £1 million sterling. Between them the syndicate had managed to realise less than one tenth of this.

Xavier was growing more eccentric and closer to egomania all the time. It is surprising that now, when everything was apparently going so well, he amazed the nurse in his dispensary by making a remark that seemed so odd, even coming from him, that she recalled it two years later.

"One day I'll end up in prison," he told her. "I know it."

But despite the occasional ominous hint—and Xavier, as they all knew, was capable of making pessimistic remarks signifying very little even in the most favourable situations—1963 was the *annus mirabilis* for the syndicate. Ménars in January; la Bouleaunière in April; Villarceaux in August; Corbeville in December—the gang's list of successes was beginning to read like a guide-book to France's great houses. And the bereaved furniture owners read like an extract from the *Almanach de Gotha* and *Bottin Mondain*—Xavier found the whole thing very funny. And the year ended on the highest note of all.

As usual the raid was immaculately planned; the date chosen,

December 31st, 1963, was perfect. St. Denis in the toughest, most proletarian section on the fringe of Paris, had the highest Communist Party membership of any area in France. On New Year's Eve it would be easier to find a monarchist than a sober man. Just before six a very large elegantly dressed man entered the cathedral in the centre of the main square. The guide started to close the doors almost as soon as he entered. It was New Year's Eve, and he wasn't going to have any idiots dawdling. The visitor asked if he was closing, and received an extremely brusque affirmative. He then amazed the guide by handing him a dozen ten franc notes (just under £10) "for the poor box". He had come a long way to see this glory of French ecclesiastical art, he went on, speaking with what the guide thought was a slight foreign accent. Could he have an extra ten minutes? There was no need for the guide to stay. He would be quite happy to lock up for him and bring the key round. He didn't want to spoil his night out.

It was all over; for that kind of tip he would have been allowed to try on the Archbishop of Paris's mitre. The stranger returned the key in due course as promised. He also wished the guide a Happy New Year, which he meant from the bottom of his heart. The cathedral had just lost its solid silver altar-piece. The affair was all the more tragic as it was a treasure that had only just been recovered after nearly a century. Three years earlier Jacques Dupont, working overtime on behalf of the Historic Monuments Department, had discovered a panel in the cellar of the cathedral. It was thirty feet long by four and a half deep, painted and horribly grimy. Dupont thought the carving looked interesting—could it be mediaeval?—and scratched the paint with his elegant thumb nail. The panel was solid silver. Not even the oldest members of the cathedral had ever seen, or heard of it. In the end Dupont assumed, for want of evidence either way, that it must have been painted over by a priest in 1870 to mislead the Prussian invaders. He did the restoration work personally on his precious find and installed it in front of the altar, a great slab of carved silver, soberly magnificent.

It must have taken at least two men, probably using a wheelbarrow, to steal the altar-piece some time after midnight on

January 1st, while the New Year's Eve parties were still going strong in the two *bistros* which encroach on the cathedral court. No one saw or heard anything; it was hardly likely they would, on that of all nights. The panel has not been seen since.

CHAPTER XIII

The Break with Xavier

One thousand nine hundred and sixty-four began on a distinctly lower key. Despite their recent successes Jean, Claude and André were all short of cash (largely because of their newly acquired extravagances). Marcel, as might be expected, spent his money with more care.

A fortnight after Christmas Claude went to the shop on the Quai Malaquais in search of a loan—his holiday expenses had been crippling. Marcel had gone out so Claude passed an hour checking through the syndicate's books, hoping to find there was some money outstanding to him. Instead he found something else, an item of almost £200 which was the cost of restoring a Louis XV table. Claude remembered that table well; he himself had stolen it, besides some notable tapestries and a selection of other valuable (and heavy) items, from Fleury-en-Bière, the Marquis de Ganay's enormous country house. Claude had thought this was one of their most dangerous operations, and he had not enjoyed the hours he had spent creeping round the endless corridors—the château had seemed as big as the Gare du Nord (it almost is).

He rang Xavier, using Marcel's phone, and asked whether they had sold the table. Xavier's irritatingly shrill voice squeaked a negative. Even after all that cash invested in disguising the piece? (which had, of course, been deducted from the total share-out). Then the explosion. Xavier airily explained that the restorations had nothing to do with disguise. When he had examined the table he had been appalled to see the feet were phoney, actually twentieth century—unbelievable, wasn't it? (The doctor was right. The old Marquis Hubert is a tweedy, red-faced figure, a spiritual refugee from those cartoons about "grouse-moor politicians" which British caricaturists used to do of the fourteenth Earl of Home and the Marquess of Salisbury. Hubert de Ganay is no aesthete. He had found the table was too low for resting his Scotch on conveniently and had cheerily ordered modern, monstrous feet to be stuck on the bottom to add height.) Xavier continued, saying that he had been very lucky; after a long search he had managed to find a set of genuine period feet. These had been fitted and Claude would be pleased to know the table was now perfectly authentic. It looked so good, Xavier added, that it seemed a shame not to keep it. Claude reacted furiously and started asking about the cost of Xavier's work on the table in greater detail. The doctor explained that it had taken three months to find the feet he needed the £200 entry included his expenses. Claude decided there was no point in prolonging the conversation. He told Xavier he was an imbecile and rang off, deciding he would go and find André. They could not allow this kind of madness to continue; it was time for a show-down.

André Huré was in the Bar Raton engaged in earnest conversation with the proprietress. He was trying to convince her that the café's decor—*style provençal*, which meant red tablecloths and earthenware wine jugs—was years out of date. Claude saw what was going on and listened attentively without interrupting André's sales pitch, which was simple but intense: a change of décor would boost trade. He had recently decorated a restaurant in the Place Dauphine and customers were now reserving tables days in advance, André went on. He had chosen "style Wild-West"—lassoes, imitation Colt .45s, "Wanted Dead or Alive" posters, an imitation colonial dresser, cheap but eye-catching, and chic . . . La patronne said she might consider the idea and moved off, leaving André a bit downcast. Claude sat down and immediately asked for a small loan; André replied that he had been about to say precisely the same thing. As Claude had suspected, times were hard all round (which was why he had got his own request in first). He started to tell the story of the Marquis de Ganay's table and noted that André was sympathetic.

In recent months Claude and Xavier had bickered over something virtually every time they came into contact and, though he admired the doctor's scholarship, André was basically on Claude's side—like him he was concerned to increase the syndicate's activity, and make more money. André was prepared to listen to any scheme that sounded as if it would be profitable, unless it was absurdly risky anyway. Claude outlined a plan he had been considering for some time and described a château he had seen at a small village called Gambais, near Houdan, a town in the Seine-et-Oise, fifty miles or so from Paris. The house was called the Château de Neuville, a name André had heard mentioned in discussions before. Claude described it and explained that it was occupied for part of the year by an American, who sometimes apparently used it to store antiques—he was in the business himself. At the moment he was abroad, in America somewhere, according to his friends, and there was no likelihood that he would return before the spring.

Meanwhile the house was wide open. No, he did not have an exact list of the contents, nor indeed any idea of what they might find. But the house was huge, and empty. There were certain to be dozens of rooms full of furniture (Claude was guessing when he said this) and if necessary they could make a whole series of trips and strip the place bare. This method, as André knew, was directly contrary to everything that Xavier had always preached, but perhaps in the circumstances it was worth trying —certainly he needed the money. The decorator was weighing the arguments on both sides when Claude, who had given a lot of thought to the conversation, delicately suggested that they should double-cross the rest of the syndicate. They might consult Marcel about getting rid of the furniture, if André could not sell it at the Hotel Rameau, but why bother about the Richiers? They could do a two-way share-out. André did not commit himself but the idea appealed sufficiently for him to say he was free right away when Claude suggested they go and look at the Château de Neuville. An hour later the Deux-Chevaux was on the road to Houdan.

*　　　*　　　*

Claude was anxious to spite Xavier, but that was not his sole reason for wishing to raid Neuville. He was seeking a solution to a problem the syndicate had faced for some time: they were beginning to run out of châteaux, or at any rate châteaux ideally suited for robbery. Because Versailles in the eighteenth century had acted as a magnet, drawing every ambitious aristocrat in the country, the Ile de France had blossomed into a breathtakingly magnificent area, with hundreds if not thousands of grand houses and elaborate gardens, all convenient for the Court, all of them inspired by the Bourbon passion for construction and decoration. But many of the houses had been destroyed after the Revolution, or allowed to rot. The Ile de France nowadays is a jumble of superior Paris suburbs; tiny towns thoroughly provincial in spirit, even though they are only an hour's train ride from the capital and, in addition, a good deal of heterogeneous industrial development, dating from the nineteenth century as well as more recently. There are still many of the original grand châteaux left as well, a testament to the reigns of those hapless, splendid and appalling Bourbons, but nothing like the number needed to keep a gang employed fortnightly over a period of years. And they had already visited all the obvious ones.

The gang was vulnerable on two fronts. There was always some chance that they might be caught *in flagrante*—if an owner returned unexpectedly, if a patrolling policeman saw a torch glow or, least likely of all, if an unusually conscientious or insomniac *gardien* jumped on them, shot-gun at the ready. But given the comparative isolation of the châteaux they selected, and the reluctance of the Paris rich to depart from a rigid pattern of life, these eventualities were fairly remote. (No member of *Le Tout Paris* would be seen dead in Paris over the weekend; equally, except during the month of August, no one would dream of being anywhere else during the week. And almost all the châteaux visited by a gang had been *residences secondaires*, inhabited two or three days a week in the summer, and not at all for the rest of the year.)

The châteaux are often so tightly crammed with heterogeneous furniture and pictures acquired by centuries of ancestors that the owners are extremely vague about what they own.

(Police called in after château thefts frequently found owners trailing bad-temperedly from room to room, gold pencils and Hermes *carnets* in hand, trying to work out precisely what had gone; in other words, whether or not the *écritoire* that used to stand in the corner had been transferred to a servant's bedroom, given to Aunt Amelie, sent to the restorers, or stolen.) No wonder the police often found it difficult to regard the thefts as important. The idea that people could treat objects of any value in such a cavalier way was incomprehensible.

Most of the things had been stolen from the aristocracy and sold to the newly rich, a precaution which meant that the true owner of an object and the syndicate's customer were not likely to come face to face. But it also led to an irritating paradox— Xavier Richier was employing his scholarship and flair to acquire exquisite things which were often sold by Marcel or Jean to customers incapable of appreciating their true value and rarity. Xavier liked things the way they were and he certainly had no intention of wasting his time by stealing anything except the very best. His system might be slow, but it was also extremely safe. In any event his own personal satisfaction stemmed entirely from selecting the very best pieces in a house, sometimes by choosing a piece the value of which the owners did not themselves appreciate until it had gone. Commercially he was wrong, but Xavier was obsessive, and not open to argument.

A handful of objects stolen by the syndicate was sold to private collectors, sometimes foreigners, who knew they must have been stolen, but this accounted for only a tiny fraction of their total turnover. Most of their customers were rich but ignorant. Many of them would probably have been content with modern reproductions still smelling of cabinet-makers' glue as long as Marcel or Jean had been clever enough to convince them that their new acquisition was, despite appearances, a couple of centuries old, and a real museum piece (which had been "restored").

Before Christmas the syndicate had met at Liévin, and Claude had taken the chance to argue that they should be less discriminating. He had suggested raids on several châteaux, Neuville among them, but Xavier had dismissed them all for one reason or another, insisting that they must continue as before, restricting themselves to the most carefully selected objects in "easy" houses. He knew about the Château de Neuville—there had been a magazine article on the place which he had filed—but he was far from impressed. The house was never open to the public so there was no way of assessing its contents accurately (the furniture illustrated in the magazine had been poor). There was also a second objection. Xavier had seen the château and his view was that it stood uncomfortably near a main road —a raid would be too risky, he pontificated, and probably fruitless as well. Claude angrily asked if he could think of anywhere better. Xavier replied that he had been studying collections of faïence but they would have to wait until he had reached a decision. Claude said the whole approach of the syndicate needed changing. They should consider an entirely new departure, like for example commissioning fake *haute époque* pieces for sale at Quai Malaquais. Xavier was furious. Claude made the scene worse by telling the offended doctor about some "get rich quick" tricks of the antiques trade. Xavier responded with a tirade in the course of which he spoke of his "vocation" to protect and restore neglected treasures of the past. Claude gave up in disgust, and left Liévin in a huff.

Commercially, he was probably in the right, a point not lost on Jean, whose own disinterested love for beauty had noticeably evaporated since he had begun to see the advantages of being rich. The 1963 successes had financed a tour of Scandinavia, an elegant Mercedes, and the decorative but expensive friend whom Jean had taken with him. He was now having to economise, which he did not enjoy, and he had never fully shared his elder brother's fantasies. Unlike Xavier, Jean had worked in the trade long enough not to have any illusions. He had also been greatly impressed by an exhibition which had been mounted in the Grand Palais on the Champs Élysées during his art school days, and on which he had been required to write a paper.

Called simply "Les Faux", the exhibition had contained an extraordinary range of exhibits of forgeries and fakes, revealing a bewildering range of human ingenuity—and dishonesty. Apart from fairly commonplace copies of Monet, Degas, Klee and Picasso, there was a small collection of fake Leonardos (including seven different versions of "La Giaconda"); a dozen spurious del Sartos; several doubtful Cranachs; and two handsome Vermeers, "The Lady at the Spinet" and "The Washing of the Hands" by Van Meegeren, the distinguished Dutch faker. Both pictures had been admired by many experts, who had never as much as questioned their authenticity and, despite the deflationary effect of the German occupation, the second fetched one and a quarter million florins, over £30,000, at an Amsterdam sale in 1943. Paintings were by no means the only forgeries on display; there were few items unrepresented, and the range extended from the obvious (bank notes and stamps) to the more arcane (fake brassware, Flemish lace, and even ivory goblets). A collection of autographed letters by the nineteenth-century French forger, Denis Vrain-Lucas, showed how easily a skilled operator can deceive even a supposedly knowledgeable client.

Vrain-Lucas produced roughly 30,000 fake letters and manuscripts between 1860 and 1870, and earned himself a comfortable fortune. Most of his wilder examples were sold to a member of the French Academy, Michel Chasles, who published a revelationary set of historical exegeses, using information from the letters as their foundation. Chasles tried to prove the chauvinist theory that Pascal, and not Newton, first discovered the laws of gravity by producing one of Vrain-Lucas's efforts. He also published new historical "evidence" based on letters Vrain-Lucas had sold him purporting to be from Sappho to Phaon; Socrates to Euclid; Caesar to Pompey; Antony to Cleopatra; Lazarus to St. Peter; Dante to Jean de Meung; Joan of Arc to the Parisians (sic); Christopher Colombus, Raphael and Amerigo Vespucci to Rabelais. Despite the intrinsic unlikelihood of anyone believing that any such correspondence could have been preserved, it took a decade—in the course of which Chasles acquired a considerable reputation as a scholar and original researcher—before Vrain-Lucas was caught. His sentence was light, in spite of the extent of his swindle; the French have always treated art crooks leniently. Vrain-Lucas was probably the most outrageous forger of all time but over the years numerous other Frenchmen have followed his example and

France can claim to be the country where faking has come near-est to attaining the stature of an art form in its own right. Antique furniture, and particularly French furniture, has for the last hundred years been the fakers' favourite territory.

Jean Richier, like everyone else in the Paris trade, knew the story of André Mailfert, and at some time or another had almost certainly bought or sold one of his products, though without knowing. Mailfert was producing fakes only forty years ago, but Jean would never have been able to pick one, and even Xavier might have been deceived by Mailfert's best work. The faker began humbly enough in 1904 when he opened a small "curi-osity shop", with borrowed money, at 73, rue Royale, in Orleans. Business was slow and when one day a local landowner asked Mailfert to restore a battered but genuine Louis XV barometer he was pleased to try his hand at something new. Mailfert was broke, but imaginative, and while working on the object he was struck by its intrinsic banality. He found it odd that this piece of carved wood should be worth 600 Francs (a present-day equivalent would be nearly £200) simply because of its antiquity. Mailfert thought that it should be possible to make an exact replica for a twentieth of this price.

His first fake cost him 37.65 Francs, of which 12 Francs went to the man who made the frame. (He was a local crafts-man who at this time made a living carving pipe bowls but later joined up with Mailfert and graduated to more ambitious items.) The only other expense was 10 Francs, for gilding. Mail-fert had been to art school and he used his own gifts as a draughtsman to inscribe on the face of his toy in faded script: "Made in Paris, at the workshops of Legrand, Court Optician . . ."

Both barometers looked very similar, so much so that a week later Mailfert had sold it for 500 Francs. His customer was a local magistrate, who also happened to be president of a club of amateur collectors and fancied his judgement. After the deal he assured Mailfert that the week-old barometer was original and that the genuine article, which had been next to it in the shop-window, was a feeble contemporary reproduction. The magistrate added that his new acquisition was a bargain but that Mailfert must expect to make mistakes while he was still a young man learning the business. The young man started to ponder.

Ten years later he owned a huge set of workshops and employed 200 craftsmen. He still made Louis XV barometers, fifty of them a week, but by then there were few Louis XV and Louis XVI items not manufactured on his premises. He retired in 1930, a millionaire several times over, and his catalogue for that year lists 800 different models of every conceivable kind of *haute époque* furniture, and contains such *jeux d'esprit* as ecclesiastical decorations of the middle ages. Mailfert devoted a lifetime to faking, with the utmost precision, an identical class of objects to those which Xavier Richier and his assistants stole.

Unlike Richier, Mailfert never came within a mile of breaking the law. He sold all his goods to dealers as reproductions (although fully aware that they themselves, who frequently despatched articles to Orleans to be copied when they lacked one chair or commode to make up a set, were certainly intending to sell the reproduction goods as antique, and at the very highest prices). Mailfert made his fortune honestly, partly because his reproductions were so good (he proudly claimed to be the inventor of various methods to give veneer an ancient, cracked look; an unbeatable system for producing worm-holes, and even authentically ancient-looking worm-excrement, in modern wood) but largely because the clients who bought his furniture from the dealers were so ignorant. By the end of a career in which he had produced, for example, approximately 30,000 "Louis XV" commodes, he claimed there was no such thing in France as a genuine one—at least, outside museums and a handful of country houses. He believed the same to be true of the Louis XV and XVI mantel-pieces with attached mirrors which his factory in Orleans had produced by the score weekly for a quarter of a century; of the Chinese Louis XVI *secrétaires* (known as "Maison Rouge" in his catalogue); of the marquetry Louis XV bureaux (style "Mazarin"); and of the *bonheurs du jour* (style "Drouot") which his workmen had painstakingly manufactured by the thousand.

Not that Mailfert was the only twentieth-century faker of French furniture, although he was almost certainly the largest, and the best. The Marché aux Puces has numerous fakers working within yards of the stands where their products are sold as authentic; many shops in the *Village Suisse* behind the Eiffel Tower have small factories attached to them (though not in the Village itself); and the rue de Charonne, where Jean Richier first developed his interest in antiques, has many scores of cabinet-makers, half of whom are faking furniture full-time, while most of the remainder combine the manufacture of fakes with "legitimate" repair and restoration work.

Claude was beginning to think they should set up an operation of this kind in parallel with the château raids. All the syndicate, except Xavier, were interested, but not even Marcel, who knew more about the subject than any of the others, had any very definite ideas about how they should begin. A raid on the Château de Neuville, however, involved no new departures. They could do it quickly and simply. It would provide them with ready cash until Xavier had finally made up his mind about the next series of raids—or they had worked out an alternative. Claude outlined his views to André in the course of the afternoon they spent unobtrusively sizing up the château. The decorator said he thought Neuville looked straightforward and they dined together in Houdan, where restaurants are cheap, to decide the details. They decided to make a night reconnaissance a couple of days later, on January 20th. If this went off well they would return one week later for the real thing.

CHAPTER XIV

The Raid on Neuville

On January 27th, André Huré, always a dashing driver, as long as the van was not carrying anything to interest the police, swung his Deux-Chevaux into an illegal parking place outside *La Palette*, in the heart of the 6th arrondissement. It stands by the angle of the rue de Seine, one of Paris's most charming streets, and the rue Jacques Callot, one of its bleakest. (Appropriately, as it is named after the nearest thing to Hogarth that France has produced; Callot is famous for his macabre drawings of the Thirty Years War). Both André and Claude were *Palette* regulars. The bar is patronised by young students; boutique owners of the quarter; beatniks and pretty foreign girls, which explained its attraction for Claude. But not tonight. He was on his own in the back parlour, known grandiloquently as the *Salle de Billiard*, eating a ham sandwich—*La Palette* relies on its free-and-easy atmosphere, not gastronomic delights, to attract the customers. Under Claude's chair was his large canvas hold-all. The two greeted each other and set off almost at once for Gambais.

By ten to seven they were heading down the Quai Voltaire from where they cut across the Pont Neuf. Then they branched west, skirting the Place de la Concorde. After the Pont de Sèvres they joined the Western Autoroute, where traffic was light; most of the commuters were already at home with their families. André cautiously put his foot down. Claude felt slightly sick but elated—as always before a raid. They drove in silence.

*   *   *

The town of Houdan boasts ruins, narrow cobbled streets, a fifteenth-century dungeon, all prominently advertised on boards outside the town, and a brace of antique shops—though not of the kind that appealed to Xavier Richier. Their speciality is country furniture of the nineteenth century, and militaria—Napoleonic shakos, rusty guns from the Franco-Prussian War, and dim nineteenth-century oils. Still Houdan looks picturesque, is in easy range of Paris, and at weekends the tortuous streets are filled with cars, the majority bearing the "75" Paris number-plate. Houdan also has a certain administrative importance: beyond a stone bridge, astride the junction of the Dreux-Fontainebleau road, stands the ugly late nineteenth-century *gendarmerie*, a tricolour flying to remind everyone that here is the central police bureau which covers an area of roughly twenty miles.

The Houdan gendarmes are consequently responsible for Gambais, a haphazard little village five miles along secondary roads to the east. The area is heavily forested, and the bungalows of Paris office-workers, who often also have apartments in the capital, stand in small rectangular plots curtained by a mature veil of oaks. And the only building in the area with any claim to architectural distinction, the sixteenth-century Château de Neuville, is also well protected by trees. The main gate is completely camouflaged and, as the house is never opened to the public, it is very little known. With its blunt, U-shaped sweep of brick and the aristocratic avenues of oaks and poplars, it is a gracious if rather unpractical building—the village joke, repeated with some awe by Gambais wives, is that the château has as many doors and windows as there are days in the year. But Neuville has charm, (it was used in 1966 as the location for a film about aristocratic life in France called *La Vie de Château*). The château is basically mediaeval but, like so many French aristocratic houses, was revamped in the eighteenth century to make it fashionable. It then belonged to Laverdy, Louis XVI's controller of finances who ended his career at the guillotine—an unduly harsh punishment for a man whose gravest fault was snobbery, though he was no genius as a financial controller. His job meant that ready cash was never a problem but he failed to make Neuville into a really important château, as the present owner, the Marquis Arnauld de la Briffe, is the first to admit. It would be a magnificent place if someone came along prepared to undertake extensive restorations at considerable cost.

The la Briffe family lived there until 1939, but the second foreign occupation in a quarter of a century proved too much both for the Château de Neuville itself, and for the family's finances. By 1945 the process of dilapidation had gone one stage too far, and the family, regretfully, is now thinking in terms of selling the place. As the present Marquise wistfully, says: "I suppose it would be ideal for a country club." In the meantime they use a few rooms in the house as a weekend retreat and for the last ten years they have let the rest of the building, consisting of about fifty rooms, to a rich, civilised and agreeable American called George Stacey, an international man of many interests. Antiques are among them, and for some years Stacey has used a handful of the marble-floored rooms for displaying furniture in the relaxed way of a man who is not scraping round for a few hundred to pay next month's rent. Several of Stacey's rooms are furnished with pleasant, though not particularly valuable, furniture that he has bought at different times because it pleased him and without any thought of resale.

*   *   *

There was only one technical problem as far as the actual question of entry was concerned. Every one of Neuville's numerous windows is shuttered; therefore Claude had equipped himself with a brace and a vice to force a shutter catch. Stowed in the back of the van they had brought a folding, ten-foot ladder in case the shuttered windows on the ground floor turned out to be too securely padlocked, and it was necessary to try a storey higher up. With the vice and the ladder Claude had also brought a pair of wire-cutters—as a connoisseur of antiques he was nothing special, but he was an expert at breaking into châteaux late at night without noise.

By eight-fifteen they were at Houdan, turning off the main

road to take Route Nationale 183, which is less impressive than
it sounds. For long stretches they followed a country lane weav-
ing between the deserted winter fields to Gambais. In the
course of a whole evening no more than half a dozen cars
usually pass this way as the road leads nowhere important, and
Houdan has no night life. Most people there watch television
and retire early. The van soon reached the section where the
road winds alongside the borders of the château's ornamental
park. Here André pulled up on a grass verge they had noted
the week before, and put the side lights out; they crossed to
the heavy, wrought iron gate which guards the rear entrance
to the house; it is an impressive sight but the fence next to it,
like everything else at Neuville, has seen better days. They had
no difficulty clambering through, and over the wide, shallow
ditch on the other side. Ahead they found an elm-lined avenue, a
couple of hundred yards long, and at the bottom the black bulk
of the château, its rounded towers silhouetted in the starlight.

Originally the château possessed a splendid moat, twenty-
five yards across, but there has been no water in it since the
nineteenth century (the young boys of the la Briffe family
like to explore the dry bottom for war souvenirs, and often come
up with half-buried jerry cans with markings of forgotten
Panzer regiments; the officers took the château over as a highly
comfortable staff headquarters in the Second World War, just
as their predecessors, the Uhlans, had done twenty-five years before). The small drawbridge is still there, but no longer serves
to keep anyone out—it can be operated easily both from the
side of the house, and from the park. It provided a useful way
for the two men to reach the back entrance without going to
the trouble of lugging their ladder and other equipment across
the dried out bottom of the moat. As in most châteaux the back
entrance is at the top of an ornamental staircase. When they
reached the top Claude broke a pane, got to work on the inside
shutter with his vice, and within a couple of minutes was letting Huré in by the door.

The two men found themselves in a Louis XIV salon sixty
feet long—the main room that Stacey had furnished for his own
use. It contained a score of assorted chairs of one kind and another, three small tables, a commode, and a pair of writing

desks, as well as an assortment of bric-à-brac. It was a better selection than Claude had secretly feared, but when they penetrated further into the house they found little else; an old library, the occasional chair here and there, and, in a small room leading off the salon, an excellent though slightly shabby Louis XV barometer, the most valuable small item in the place. They left it, through ignorance. The problem was what to take. Claude indicated the one set of chairs in the salon, eight apparently Louis XVI *chaises cannées*, and said decisively: "These are the best." They hauled them back to the van, Claude carrying two at a time without any trouble, but André straining a bit. Working without a break for an hour and a half they removed almost the entire contents of the salon (a system Xavier would have despised) and piled their haul in some bushes as near as they could get to the van. The total, apart from the set of oval backed chairs, consisted of three Louis XVI *bergères*; a pair of copper fire-dogs; three *écritoires*; and various other items chosen at random.

They were both breathing heavily, half exhausted, and as usual half frightened, despite their long experience.

They paused for a moment under the elms. André smoked a cigarette while Claude ate the ham sandwich he had brought in the hope of calming his stomach which, as he knew, was certain to give him trouble during the job. When he had finished, he thoughtlessly threw the paper away—it bore the address: Jambon Saint Charles, 129 bis, rue Saint Charles, Paris XV—two minutes' walk from his wife's flat in the rue de la Croix Nivert, a fact noted by the police a couple of days later.

They had to take a decision because the small station wagon could not hold even half the contents of the *salon*. A basic rule of the antique trade is that a set of anything is vastly more valuable than a piece in isolation. Following this they loaded the eight matching Louis XVI *chaises* into the van and left the odd chairs, the *écritoires* and the rest of the items, fairly well-hidden in the scrub on the park side of the ditch. They had just finished when the evening began to go badly wrong.

A Renault 403 appeared from the direction of Houdan—the first vehicle of any kind they had seen. It turned its headlights on full and drew to a halt in front of them. They were too professional to consider trying to run for it. They stayed where they were.

Two *gendarmes* got out, Maxime Laparra and Jean St. Sever, both from the Houdan squad. Claude promptly started fiddling with the nearside back light. André understood, smiled at the *flics*, shrugged helplessly, and put on his most masculine voice.

"Back light keeps going out."

"What've you got in the van?" asked Laparra.

"Just a few old chairs."

"Chairs?"

"Yes, we're decorators. We picked them up from Vert Galant and we're delivering them to a restorer in Rueil-Malmaison— he's called Guy Bunau-Varilla. You can check easily enough— if you think it's worth the bother." Considering how terrified he was, André felt it had come out pretty well.

"Papers."

They looked all right—the profession was given as decorators. Laparra, a squat, inarticulate little man with a blue chin, noted the details down laboriously:

"Huré, André—Decorator—6, Place Dauphine, Paris 6.

"Mabilotte, Claude—Decorator—215, rue de la Croix Nivert, Paris 15.

"Interrogated west exit of Château de Neuville, 10.30 p.m. Driving a Citroën Deux-Chevaux 7541 JM 75. Everything in order."

Claude, dressed respectably as usual, appeared smiling. "I think it'll get us home now. It's just a faulty contact."

In France, as in England, working-class policemen tend to be cautious when dealing with obvious members of the educated middle-class. As they later explained to their superiors: "We noticed they had furniture in the wagon, but they were decorators, so it was logical."

"They spoke very well, very politely, you could see they were educated people."

The police drove off in one direction towards Houdan, the decorators in the other. Claude swore with great passion and creativity. André was trembling. He asked what they should do. Claude gave the sensible answer. They must return to the château and replace all the stolen furniture.

They drove into the forest, almost a mile away, and sneaked back to the west exit, stumbling through the undergrowth. They did not dare follow the road in case the police drove back.

"Thank Christ," Claude said, when they arrived back at the point where they had been interrogated. "They've gone."

"Round to the front of the château in the car—we can see if they've been making inquiries at the big house." They returned to the van, sufficiently confident now to walk cautiously along the roadside. They drove round to the front of the house. What happened then was like a comedy sequence from a twenties film. They came cautiously up the drive, their headlights off, and suddenly saw two big *black* cars parked in the U-shaped court in front of the château. "Back, back," shouted Claude. André slid to a halt, skidding on the mud and cobbled track. He reversed like a rally driver. The van took the Paris road, André's foot flat on the floor-board. Claude was still cursing— it was beginning to sound like the liturgy of a Black Mass. Eventually Claude calmed down enough to listen to André who was gibbering about road blocks, dumping the chairs, his friend Bunau-Varilla at Reuil, and a first class lawyer, in an incoherent, terrified stream.

"Stop here."

André pulled up so sharply that Claude was thrown against the dash-board. He was still complaining as he threw the last of the eight chairs into a ditch thirty yards from the edge of the forest, and André, working by torchlight, covered them with leaves and branches. It was just nine miles from Neuville. (In the circumstances they did a fair job; the chairs were not discovered until May 19th—three and a half months later.)

André was sure that his influential friend and protector Guy "Bruno" Bunau-Varilla would somehow sort things out—he had known the older man for many years, and at one time had worked as his secretary in a grand office in the Avenue du President Wilson. (This was before Bunau-Varilla, like Marcel Bihn, had "political" troubles, and was forced into temporary retirement.) André still received a regular monthly allowance from "Bruno", who was sixty-five, and whom he regarded as a father. Claude was more sceptical—he was trying to work out whether the two cars outside the château had definitely been from the Seine-et-Oise police. They had driven off so fast that he could not be sure—maybe if they returned they would still be able to get the furniture back where it came from, except, of course, for those eight chairs. Suddenly they both saw a set of red lights ahead; a road block perhaps. There was nothing wrong with André's reflexes, particularly when stimulated by fear. For the second time that night, he about-turned the old Deux-Chevaux, headed for the Chartres-Paris road, and then cut across country. It took them four hours via back roads to reach firstly the sleeping town of Savigny-sur-Onge and then Rueil-Malmaison.

By now they were both exhausted but a shade more optimistic. Claude thought it unlikely that the robbery would be discovered for several days and was wondering whether to go back the next night and pick up the chairs in the forest and the furniture near the gate. André was convinced that Bunau-Varilla would find a way out. When they reached Villa Le Malikran, Bunau-Varilla's new address, they left the car and knocked.

But it had been a night of misjudgements for both of them. The chairs were simply nineteenth-century copies of Louis XVI oval-backed *chaises*, which Stacey had bought because he needed to fill space in Neuville. He had thought them something of a bargain, too. They had cost him precisely three hundred dollars (£100); if the decorators had been lucky they might have got four hundred and fifty (£150) for them. The role of Xavier Richier had been justified.

And they were also wrong about the likelihood of the theft being discovered.

Before they had even arrived at Rueil, Henri Guerini, chief of the Gambais *gendarmerie*, had made two telephone calls from his tiny office overlooking the Dreux-Fontainebleau road. The first had been to the Seine-et-Oise Brigade H.Q. at Nantes la Jolie, to ask for instructions. He had listened attentively to his captain, made some notes, and then, highly pleased with himself and his *gendarmes*, St. Sever and Laparra, had called the Paris *Brigade des Recherches* at Exelmans. He asked for the Commandant, and told the whole story.

"Yes, my men—" he emphasised "my" lightly, "decided to take another look after these two decorators left. They found—" Guerini began to read in an expressionless drone—"footprints in front of the gate leading to the western exit of the château. In a ditch approximately thirty-five metres due east there were three, what's this, oh yes, *fauteuils*—" he spelled the word out and then his voice rose triumphantly—"a ten-foot folding ladder, and a canvas bag containing *a complete housebreaker's kit*. There were a pair of pliers; they were black, as a matter of fact, a large wrench with a red wooden handle, trade mark 'Valdor', number 'A stroke . . .'"

The captain interrupted Guerini's triumphant catalogue and said all he wanted was the names—the other details could be noted the following day, by the G.R.B. in Paris. Guerini was delighted at the opportunity of a trip to the capital to demonstrate the efficiency of the Houdan police. He said he would bring St. Sever along, in case someone needed to be identified.

Although the captain offered no congratulations, which he had half hoped for, Guerini went to bed a very satisfied policeman. But not before calling St. Sever with the good news and orders to report for duty at seven a.m.—and not a second later.

CHAPTER XV

The First Arrests

Any passer-by would have thought they had come from an all night orgy. They were pale, unshaven, exhausted and dispirited. André pulled up outside the breathtaking and invariably unnoticed romanesque façade of St. Germain des Pres, the next morning. It was eleven a.m. and citizens with clear consciences, who had bathed and breakfasted respectably at eight, were drinking mid-morning coffee across the Square at the Deux Magots. André was plunged into uncomprehending despair; "Bruno" had let them down. He had been apologetic, but said he was on the point of leaving for a trip. As for a lawyer, Claude was certain that "Bruno" knew no one suitable, and would have been reluctant to help them even if he had; his attitude had actually been mildly censorious. Claude felt a kind of sour satisfaction at having his pessimistic predictions on the subject fulfilled. But, at least, they had worked out an alibi, of sorts. André dropped Claude, hurriedly cut down to his flat at 20, rue Dauphine, and transferred six chairs, unfortunately all he had on the premises, into the van. Carrying them almost killed him.

He then weaved his way through the lunchtime traffic to a *tapissier* and restorer he knew, Ernest Lamour, at 88, rue du Cherche-Midi.

André ordered his six chairs to be painted grey-white, the same colour as the ones at Gambais. As they were grotesquely crude 1960 copies in the Jacob style, which he and Mabilotte

119

had hoped to palm off on some innocent, Lamour wondered why he was wasting money on them. But when he heard what Huré was prepared to pay for a rush job he shrugged and accepted. All decorators were mad anyway. If this one wanted to chuck his money away on rubbish, that was his affair.

André repeated on four separate occasions that once they were completed he wanted them transported to his friend Bunau-Varilla—he gave Lamour a careful note of the address. Then, convinced he had done all he could, he headed for home—and bed. He was ready to drop.

There is a courtyard at 20, rue Dauphine. As he entered, André saw two men in khaki raincoats and a uniformed *gendarme* standing with their backs to him on the other side, hammering on the Concierge's door. Huré turned tail and ran.

It was a great day for Henri Guerini. At the Exelmans Station he stood grandly beside St. Sever, while the Commandant detailed two of his best men, Gendarmes Lerouge and Chambrion, to arrest the decorators from rue Dauphine and 215, rue de la Croix Nivert. Then he listened to the Commandant talking to the great Commissaire Chevalier himself.

But Huré and Mabilotte, it emerged as the day wore on, had disappeared. The Concierge at rue Dauphine was sure André had not returned since the previous afternoon; Monique said, quite truthfully, that she hadn't seen Claude since January 25th, when he had come to visit the child, and promised money —soon.

But Guerini's big day was not yet over. A message came through to the Central Search Office of the Police Judiciaire at Romainville that Huré might have gone to hide at his mother's house in Puteaux. With St. Sever and Adjutant Marsegne of the G.R.B., who said that Chevalier had made the two men's arrest a top priority, they raced to this suburb of Paris. But Huré was not at home; his parents, Albert and Cecile Huré, were clearly telling the truth when they said unhappily that it was months since they had seen their son.

The black 403 called at the Puteaux *gendarmerie* in search of a new lead. The pink, middle-aged face of the local *gendarme* grew even pinker with excitement, when Marsegne asked if the name André Huré meant anything to him.

"Huré, have you got him?" The station officer was already producing his notebook.

"No, but we will."

"Marvellous, if anyone ever had it coming to him . . . That Huré—" the officer struggled to find words expressive enough.

"You know him then?"

"Know him—by God, he's the most diabolical villain in Puteaux. If I could get my hands on André Huré for five minutes . . ."

Marsegne, who had already checked that the decorator had no previous convictions, looked puzzled. Guerini swelled with pride. If his station at Gambais had been instrumental in catching a criminal as important as this . . . visions of commendations, even promotion, ran through his head.

"What's Huré been up to?" Marsegne asked.

"I've been trying to get him since—" the station officer checked his book—"since February 16th, 1962, nearly two years."

"Yes?" Marsegne was getting restive.

"He owes the Puteaux Court one hundred and ninety-eight francs and fifty centimes, that's all. The wicked bastard jumped a red light—I arrested him myself as a matter of fact, and we've been trying ever since to get hold of him to collect the fine."

It was hard on Guerini's fantasies, but made little difference to the G.R.B. They arrested Huré the following day, January 29th. Claude Mabilotte, who had gone underground with the aid of some friends in the Place de la Nation, eventually decided he might as well get it over with, too—he couldn't carry on in Paris with every *flic* in town carrying his picture, and when he had turned to the Richiers for aid to leave the country, they had told him unsympathetically that he had only himself to blame.

They could give him £2,000. He thought about it day in and day out. Where could he take off to—North Africa? Italy? There was nowhere he could be sure of supporting himself, honestly or otherwise. His life, his friends, his business contacts, everything that mattered to him was in Paris. He decided there was no way out. And on February 10th, he gave himself up to the police.

Hoping it might count in his favour, he promptly made a full confession to the Château de Neuville theft, doing all he could to make Huré sound like the leading spirit. As for himself, he tried to sound naïve, of lower intelligence than Huré, easily led, and reluctantly sucked into a criminal vortex through a combination of inanition and neurotic inadequacy. He would have been depressed to know that when Chevalier saw his statement he laughed heartily, shaking his head, and dropping the ash of his Gitane on to his already maltreated jacket.

When Huré was shown Mabilotte's confession on February 12th, he saw what was going on, and promptly changed his original statement about the Lamour chairs (he had insisted these were the ones that had been in the van at Neuville) hoping it wasn't too late to play down his own personal role, as Claude had done. Not that the police were too worried about the confessions one way or another. As far as Neuville went, Chevalier had enough evidence to convict both men several times over.

Huré's alibi of the chairs had evaporated as soon as St. Sever was taken to Lamour. He examined the six (not eight) chairs Huré had delivered so hastily on the day after the robbery, and pronounced without hesitation and with a wealth of conclusive detail that they were not the same ones he had examined in the van that night on Route 183.

Monsieur Viger, the *Régisseur*, identified the *bergères* and *bonheurs du jour* in the ditch as being from the château; so did Monsieur Raynaud, an antique dealer and friend of George Stacey, from Houdan, who also, acting with the authority of the American who had telephoned instructions from New York, preferred charges against the two decorators. Clearly, confessions or not, Claude and André were finished.

But the château gang (to which neither made any reference in their statements)?

Chevalier had been convinced from the start that Mabilotte was the gang's break-in specialist. Huré, he guessed, was a regu-

lar *homme de main*, who probably also disposed of property he
had stolen to dealers via his contacts in Versailles at the Hotel
Rameau. When the police, accompanied by the Neuville
Régisseur, Viger, had examined the method of entry they had
reported two facts. The burglar had originally started to drill a
thirty millimetre hole in the window-frame (after forcing the
outside shutter). He had then apparently decided for some
reason that it was unnecessarily large; his final hole, through
which he had passed the long screwdriver to open the latch,
had been sixteen millimetres.

As well as being otherwise identical in all details to a score
of unsolved cases on the G.R.B. files, the two diameters were
also the same as those used on every other occasion. For a court
it was hardly conclusive evidence—drills, after all, come in
standard diameters. But it was enough to convince Chevalier.

Then came a bizarre development in the case. A fortnight
before their scheduled trial—at the Versailles Correctional
Court on March 10th—Mabilotte's lawyer, Maître Hayot, wrote
to Staccy, now back at the Château de Neuville. His client,
Hayot movingly explained, had behaved foolishly—as boys will
the world over. He had made a full confession but still had one
thing on his conscience: Stacey's eight missing chairs. If he had
been able to remember exactly where they had left them, he
would naturally have furnished all indications. But he was not
a professional criminal; this weak lad had been overcome by
panic, and he could only recall that they had been driving east
for twenty minutes or so before they stopped, and found the
ditch. In the circumstances, would Monsieur Stacey be so good
as to get a dealer who had seen the chairs to furnish a valuation?
Naturally, it would be paid immediately and in full.

Stacey promptly telephoned Maître Hayot to discuss the
matter and mentioned that apart from Monsieur Raynaud, his
dealer friend from Houdan (*who had actually preferred the
charges in his own absence*) he could not think of a dealer off-
hand who was qualified to make a retrospective valuation. Still
he would try to come up with someone; perhaps he had some
photographs somewhere. And also he would try to find his original bill. As far as he could remember he had actually paid . . .
but at this point, Maître Hayot stopped him short.

"No need to go into all that," he said.

Despite his involvement with Stacey, Monsieur Raynaud would be entirely acceptable as a valuer. Would he let the lawyer have his assessment as soon as possible (and, of course, enclose a statement of his fee for the job).

Raynaud, who has a Gallic acuteness about cash, reckoned this was a gift from God. Adding a mental (and unstated) percentage for the inconvenience, he sent a valuation of 900 dollars, exactly three times what Stacey had originally paid, as Raynaud knew.

The same morning, Hayot called the American and asked him to collect his cash. Stacey, a bit puzzled about the amount (as Raynaud with professional punctiliousness had omitted to tell him about the inflated valuation), went round to the distinguished lawyer's exquisitely furnished offices at 68, rue Ampère, off the Place Pereire, the same afternoon. He left with a profit of two hundred per cent.

It was very odd, thought Chevalier, particularly as Hayot was probably the smartest criminal lawyer in France (eighteen months later he was to make a sensational appearance in the Ben-Barka trial, defending the two French drug squad police accused of kidnapping the Moroccan Socialist Leader in broad daylight on the Boulevard St. Germain).

Why had Hayot been eager to accept a clearly biased valuer? And pay so promptly?

Chevalier drove down to Pontoise prison at 7, Avenue Victor Hugo to talk to Mabilotte. The tough decorator looked acutely unhappy.

"You want a quick sentence before we produce any evidence about the château gang, don't you, Claude?"

"Don't know what you mean."

Chevalier got his cigarette going well and settled down equably to asking the same set of questions again and again.

He repeated the interrogation at daily intervals.

"Does the tapestry of St. Gervais mean anything to you? Have you ever been to Le Mans? Where did you say you spent the Christmas before last?"

Claude stuck determinedly to one story only—he had been in the Ardèche, in a cottage he and his wife had borrowed from a friend. He described the cottage in detail, which was easy enough as it actually existed, and he had stayed there on many occasions. As for his wife, Claude believed, quite correctly, that the police would get nothing useful out of her. The friend was in Tunis, as the police discovered when they checked at the Ardèche cottage. Claude was not worried even if they traced him; on principle, apart from personal feelings, he would undoubtedly refuse to say anything. Claude was lying about the cottage, but not about the Laval and Le Mans raids. He had not been there and had always assumed Jean or Xavier had removed the two tapestries. But he didn't know for certain. It was stalemate in one way, though after a couple of weeks of interrogation, both he and Chevalier had reached a point of at least tacit understanding. Chevalier knew Claude was one of the men he was after, though clearly not the most important one—it was evident that he simply did not know enough about antiques to plan such subtle thefts, or select items with such discrimination. Claude in turn knew the point Chevalier had reached; there was no evidence linking him with the château gang, except circumstantially—the method of entry.

But if Chevalier decided to be awkward, he could probably keep them both in prison at Pontoise until the autumn, before they were as much as brought to trial. French law can be unbelievably dilatory; if he really got nasty, that persistent cop, with his grinding questions (he seemed to be as well informed about the château raids as Mabilotte himself), could keep them in custody for at least nine months, "because the police are still pursuing their inquiries". Over the weeks, with Chevalier concentrating on Mabilotte and virtually ignoring Huré, Hayot became certain that this was the police plan.

Yet there was no indication that the trial was going to be delayed. With ten days to go, Hayot produced a finesse, without much hope that it would come off. He informed the Court that Mabilotte would plead guilty and throw himself on their mercy. He was not a professional criminal, had made full and generous restitution to the man he had burgled, and would be presenting a medical certificate from a doctor and a psychiatrist testifying that a combination of life in prison and his bitter chagrin at his own fall from grace, made his immediate freedom—"on health grounds"—imperative. It sounded hopeless but no one could accuse Maître Hayot of not being a trier.

Claude could only hope, but Hayot, and his colleague, Maître Grand'Bac, had warned him that it was a hundred to one chance against him being freed. He began to feel desperation faced with the undefined prospect of prison; and Chevalier's reiterated questions were driving him mad. So when he appeared in the familiar haze of smoke four days before the trial was due, Claude felt his stomach turn over.

The Commissaire was in high good humour.

"It's virtually all over," he began, beaming.

Chevalier, fixing him with that unshifting, attentive gaze he had come to dread, continued to grin like an old cat. He offered a cigarette, it had become part of their ritual, but his eyes still never left Mabilotte.

"Now, *mon vieux*, let me tell you all about it. Firstly, I've decided you're not such a desperate villain as all that and my heart bleeds for you constricted in here.

"Anyway, what I'm going to do is bring joy to your heart and that of your admirable lawyer. On March 10th I intend to support your appeal for *'liberté provisoire'* on, what are the grounds now? Ah, yes, 'health reasons'. Very good that.

"Incidentally, tell Maître Hayot how much I enjoyed his letter to Monsieur Stacey, the delightful American you robbed; I'm sure you remember him. That bit about 'lads will be lads the world over' was particularly true, I thought. Tell the Maître he should have been a literary man, his talents are quite wasted at the Bar."

"I don't know what you're going on about, Monsieur le Commissaire," said Claude, quite truthfully. "Why are you helping me?"

"I've told you," said Chevalier, heading for the door and politely leaving the Gitanes on the table. "I've decided you're not a bad lad anyway—" he paused urbanely as the jailer cluttered along the stone corridor to open the cell from the outside —"and I think you might be able to help me."

And he had gone away, whistling.

At the trial, Maître Grand'Bac, Hayot's colleague, pleaded as expected. He claimed eloquently that Mabilotte was young and foolish, not criminal. He asked for *"liberté provisoire"* and produced his medical certificates. The prison authorities in turn produced an assessment from their psychiatrist—neither Huré nor Mabilotte were abnormal, he reported. Moreover, they were both aware of the consequences of their actions.

Then came a bad moment for Claude. His previous record was produced. Apart from the usual minor motoring offences there was something more important, which did not help his lawyer's insistence that as far as crime went, he was an *ingénue*. On May 10th, 1960, he had been convicted of a whole string of offences by the Seine Tribunal: the most serious was robbery, the others included forgery of a driving licence. These 1960 offences had been Mabilotte's first and according to French law first offenders are almost invariably sentenced *avec sursis*: that is, their punishment is suspended on condition that they do not appear again. However, the Tribunal had taken the line that despite his previous good record, these offences were sufficiently serious to merit a *ferme* sentence of fifteen months, which he had served in full.

The President and his two fellow judges looked grave; then Chevalier spoke. The police, he said, would be very concerned at Huré being freed. As for Mabilotte they accepted his poor medical condition, and would have no objection to his being allowed *"liberté provisoire"* if the court saw fit.

Finally, the whole case was adjourned; Huré was to remain in prison until a final trial when all the evidence could be presented. Mabilotte had certain formalities to go through, but he could expect to be released in the course of a couple of months and would remain on probation until the second trial. Chevalier had swung it. Claude was returned to the cells, delighted and amazed.

When he thanked Grand'Bac, the lawyer remarked that it was Commissaire Chevalier who had made the crucial difference.

"You ought to thank him."

The Commissaire soon appeared; Mabilotte looked at him suspiciously.

"You ought to be careful you don't waste your best years cooped up in some dump like this."

Mabilotte, who could not have agreed more passionately, contented himself with a non-committal grunt; he was trying to work out what Chevalier was building up to.

"There's one disadvantage of probation. It means you can be hauled in at any time, and you have to report regularly to the local Commissariat. I'm sure the sergeant explained it all to you."

"Yes."

"And, of course, in many ways it's actually preferable to be tried for all your offences at the same time."

"All what offences?"

"Don't get excited, you'd do better to listen. When a man has committed several crimes, but not confessed to more than one or two, we can pick him up every time we get new evidence, have him put away, and then re-arrest him again as soon as he is released. We call it the yo-yo method."

For a second, the big man felt panic. Then he told himself Chevalier would never get on to Xavier.

"If you get new evidence, yes, I suppose you could do that," he said.

"We always get evidence in the end, son," said Chevalier. "But I'm not worried. This furniture stealing business, it's all very well but apart from the owners—*they* naturally always get very worked up about their dirty old chairs—no one is going to lose much sleep. Only a handful of people are affected and as you ought to know, you're a bit of an expert on all this, aren't you, almost all this aristocratic furniture has already been stolen at some time or another in the past. That's usually how their ancestors got hold of all the junk in the first place, isn't it?"

Chevalier broke off to laugh. Mabilotte sat tight, fixing him with his dark eyes and wondering when he was finally going to come to the point, whatever it was going to be. And also how soon he was going to be free. He wished Hayot was there.

"On the face of it, this château gang stuff looks bad in the papers, you know. '*NF. 14,000 (£10,000) commode stolen from Duke's château*', all this kind of thing. But I often wonder who'd be mad enough to pay that kind of money for a bit of old furniture, don't you?"

Chevalier paused for an answer, then carried on equably against the silence.

"But objects belonging to the State now, that's a different matter altogether. Especially since Malraux became Minister (of Cultural affairs). You can't move nowadays without some official or another screaming about the loss of France's national patrimony. This nonsense at Laval and Le Mans. And the silver altar-piece your people thought they were so smart to steal from St. Denis. We can't have people going around stealing things like that, worth millions, as if they're shop-lifting in Monoprix. You've no idea the trouble that thing has caused us. And where the hell do your friends think they're going to get rid of that Le Mans tapestry? I tell you this, if they think they can steal things like that for their own amusement and make everybody look like an idiot, they'd better think again. You just pass the word around."

"I don't know what you're talking about."

"Maybe not—but let me give you some advice. I've done you a good turn, now do yourself one. If you don't know all about the château gang, which I don't believe, find out quick.

"You've got two entrics on your record now—and we can get you any time we feel like it. I could get you five years as easily as that," Chevalier snapped his fingers. "Remember, five years next time."

"There's not going to be a next time."

"That, Claude, *mon vieux*, depends entirely on you."

CHAPTER XVI

The Prodigal's Return

The G.R.B., whose triumph it had been finally to lay hands on two important château robbers after so long, were collectively puzzled, and outraged, at the idea of one of them walking off a free man, even provisionally. As soon as he got back from the trial the Commissaire ordered a meeting of the whole team.

"At one stage I thought André Huré was *prêt à grimper au mur*." (In police argot, at breaking point and ready to make a full confession.)

Chevalier had chosen as the moment of maximum strain February 12th, the day Huré had found himself confronted with Claude's confession, and was then driven in a closed police van to the *Identité Judiciaire* H.Q. in order to *passer au piano* —have his fingerprints taken.

"But Huré is a lot tougher than he looks—he stood up to it all a lot better than Mabilotte. So I decided Claude's our man, and he is.

"The first thing he's going to do is try and get the tapestries back—if they haven't been sold abroad, which I doubt. So we'll have to see where he goes. Joseph," he turned to le Bruchec, "You're in charge of the *filature* of Mabilotte. He's no use to us in prison, he might lead us somewhere when he gets out. We've got plenty of time to make other arrangements for him as well."

At a later date the Commissaire referred to these "arrangements".

"It was a long, difficult affair for us," he said. "And in some cases one has no choice but to resort to uncivilised methods." He gestured sadly, and produced an expression of deliberately unconvincing comic despair. He was, his expression said, the victim of a deplorably squalid vocation.

When Claude Mabilotte was finally released from Pontoise Prison late in April his telephone had been bugged; so had his flat.

They let Claude go at seven a.m. and after a short chat with his lawyer he felt strangely lonely, and disorientated. Already he had drifted into prison routine. Outside everyone seemed to be rushing madly towards some goal, while he had nothing. He hesitated outside a café and then decided to keep on the move—whatever he was aiming for, he supposed he would be nearer to it if he didn't hang about.

The obvious thing was to visit his wife in the rue de la Croix Nivert, if she was there. She wasn't. There was only a cold apartment, a lot of dirty crockery in the sink, some unopened bills, a sense of quiet desolation. The beady-eyed *concierge*, her gaze at once hostile and contemptuous behind heavy cheap glasses, finally condescended to inform him that Monique had taken their child and gone to stay with her mother at Puteaux, outside Paris.

"If you wanted to see her," she continued nastily, "you could go there."

Claude turned his back on her and outside on the pavement was careful to avert his face as he passed the neighbouring leather shop which belongs to M. Dupuy, who is also proprietor of the flats at number 215. Chances were he would be even more unfriendly than that old cow of a *concierge*; ex-prisoners are not exactly fêted in respectable blocks of Paris flats.

And the Fifteenth arrondissement, where Mabilotte had lived on and off for eight years, is nothing if not respectable. In Paris terms the Fifteenth is the poor man's Seventh; it is what Hendon is to Hampstead. The rue de la Croix Nivert, one of the *quartier*'s main arteries, begins not far from the glittering new

UNESCO building in Place Fontenoy, and from there continues east-west as far as the Porte de Versailles and the Parc des Expositions. The further it goes, the more residential and dull it becomes. Claude reckoned there was little to commend it; no hint of gaiety, nothing remotely adventurous or *louche*, though it was, in spite of everything, conveniently placed for château-visiting trips to the Ile de France. The buildings are large, sometimes even massive, but they have none of the grandeur of the eighteenth-century residences in the Seventh. The concrete apartment blocks, mainly dating from the twenties, are perfectly adequate machines for living in, solid and respectable as a fifty pound note, but without grace. They are protected with great symmetrical doors of steel and glass, bristling with electrical gadgets for keeping unauthorised visitors out. Every *concierge* has a notice on her door warning hawkers and salesmen that they are not wanted.

Claude was again in this street that had never seemed so hostile. Yet it was one of those clear mornings of Paris spring, and as he walked, unthinkingly following what had been a regular morning itinerary in happier days, he started to feel better. At least he was free. He must get down to planning how he could avoid going back, ever. Involuntarily, for that was the way he had always been accustomed to go, he brushed right off the Boulevard. (So too did the man following him very slowly in a Renault R8 at a distance of 100 yards.)

Where, he wondered, could the decorator be making for? First 200 yards down the Boulevard, then the right turn into the quiet side streets, then another turn, this time left, and on to the next main street, the rue de Vaugirard. Inspector Joseph le Bruchec, following in his Renault, was a lot more content than Claude; this was the kind of police work he enjoyed, particularly after the long spell when he had been spending three-quarters of his life in the Faubourg St. Honoré office, sifting through endless dusty files of robberies and examining sepia photographs of *haute époque* furniture. Mabilotte's route was curious; perhaps he was going somewhere important.

Claude walked on, briskly but evidently preoccupied, and le Bruchec wondered for a moment whether he might actually be heading for the Local Police Commissariat in the rue Blomet.

But he suddenly swung left into the picturesquely named rue
Thèophraste Renaudot (he was a distinguished seventeenth-
century doctor), and came out at the bottom in the Square St.
Lambert, the prettiest section of the whole *quartier*. Again le
Bruchec brightened; perhaps the big man was going to meet his
girl-friend.

The Parc St. Lambert is a curious survival from the 1920s, so
much so that it might easily have been used as a back-drop for
a film by the very young René Clair. There is a pond for sailing
toy boats and a brace of roundabouts—a questionable advantage
from the point of view of the young mothers who use the Parc
as a regular meeting place every fine day, because rides cost
money. On the other side of the Parc there is a built-up concrete section (the Fifteenth is over-run by concrete) where the
older boys play football and a game resembling fives which they
have invented for themselves using the concrete buttresses. From
here there are steps leading first back to the Parc, and then into
the perimeter of the Square itself. Claude Mabilotte had liked to
wander around here on fine days, working on his suntan, and
showing more interest in the mothers than in their exigent
children, whose pleadings for roundabout money were the one
discomfort of the place. Now he settled down and smoked a
cigarette (he was still at the immediately post-prison stage when
every smoke seemed like an act of luxuriant self-indulgence).
The scene could hardly have suited the swarthy policeman less
and hovering incongruously by the pond he managed to be
highly conspicuous. Claude never glanced behind him. He was
thinking about his plan for survival.

Obviously, the thing that was really worrying Chevalier was
the mediaeval tapestry from Le Mans—typical of the Richiers
to go for something with no possible resale value, and endless
trouble attached to it. Supposing he got it back? And could he
claim the credit? If only he could implicate the Richiers, but
if he did all his thefts over the years would come out. He would
get three years. He got up and headed back. Joseph le Bruchec
attracted some surprised attention as he set off at an athletic
sprint diagonally across the Parc towards his Renault. Claude
noticed nothing.

Outside his apartment he hesitated whether to go up or not,

and finally, quite unconsciously, made a fateful decision. The emptiness, and the dirty crockery, were too depressing. Instead he would have a drink and phone from the café. He turned into the "Auberge des Provinces de France", twenty yards or so down the street, and exchanged a few words with the *patron*. Claude drank a *pastis*, the first alcohol since when, yes of course, that red wine in *La Palette* on the evening of January 27th, so far away.

In the "Auberge des Provinces de France" there is no coin-box system; for the telephone one simply enters a small alcove without a door between the bottom end of the bar, the lavatory, and a second dining-room in the rear. The *patron* connects the line from the bar, and you pay him 50 centimes after you have got through. Anyone in the rear dining-room, or even at the end of the bar furthest away from the door, can easily overhear all conversations.

Unfortunately for them, the *Groupe pour la Repression du Banditisme* do not have at their disposal the resources enjoyed by, say, S.D.E.C.E., one of the French espionage bureaux, which has its headquarters in the so-called "Swimming Pool" building near the Élysée Palace. Here they sometimes seem to have a team of *standardistes* recording half the conversations in Paris, made from both private lines and public phones. But where the S.D.E.C.E. would have tapped every bar in the *quartier* the G.R.B. had contented themselves with fitting a listening device to Claude's personal line. Accordingly, through no fault of their own, they missed a conversation that would have saved them almost precisely twelve months' work. "Telephone." Mabilotte gestured to the alcove and the *patron* made the connection. Claude dialled VOL-16-08, and to his relief the unmistakable gruff, off-key voice of Jean Richier said "Allo, oui?" at the other end.

Out in the car discreetly parked across the street, Joseph le Bruchec was completing his notes of Mabilotte's morning itinerary and recording the name "Auberge des Provinces de France" for future reference. He had decided against following Claude into the bar—he expected to be shadowing him for several days, and wanted to delay for as long as possible the moment when Claude noticed his face for the first time.

"It's Claude."

"Claude, when did you get out? Xavier's furious, he says—"

Mabilotte cut in. "You can tell him this, straight away. We've got to get that —— of a tapestry back to Le Mans, today if possible."

"But . . ."

"No 'buts'. It's got to be back there in the cathedral by the end of the week, and if it isn't I'll be round to see to you personally. I don't know why you were ever so mad as to touch the thing. Couldn't you guess how the police would react—they'd do anything to get it back. And listen, I need some money, say twenty thousand francs. If you don't want the cops to hear about Liévin you'd better have it waiting for me at *La Palette* by noon tomorrow. I'm going to get out of Paris. Tell Xavier . . . you understand?"

Jean, now stammering, tried to get some more information, but Claude had already rung off. He paid for his *pastis*, made a brief sortie to the garage down the road to order a service for his Fiat, and went back to the apartment to pack.

A week later Xavier Richier made a trip to Paris carrying his overnight case and a present for his mother, a rug which he had wrapped with great care in several layers of brown paper, a lot of string, and numerous strips of sticky tape. The parcel was so heavy that the little doctor had trouble in carrying it; he accordingly asked his colleague, Dr. Edouard Westeel, to drive him and his present to the station at Lens.

"The Sacristan cried when the tapestry arrived," recalled Canon Mabon, from Le Mans, his voice glowing with emotion and joy, even a year later. "It was beautifully packed and had been sent, express and with the carriage prepaid, from the Gare d'Austerlitz. We were all deeply moved. It was just like the return of the Prodigal Son. There can be no doubt—it was a gift from God."

A pious theory from the good canon. But even if the deity had been responsible for the young man in dark glasses who arrived at the "Consigne" desk at the station one night it would be sacrilegious to saddle the Almighty with the unholy joke he perpetrated. The man was called Claude Saudeville, a friend of

Jean Richier's, and he had no idea what he was doing. Though indeed there had nearly been a religious aspect to the affair, of a sort anyway. Jean, at his most emotional, had fancied a grand gesture. His idea was to go to the great cathedral and return the tapestry in person—though only after he had received assurance that he was protected by the seal of the confessional. Jean thought the idea a stroke of genius. He would have calmed Chevalier down, and also have received absolution into the bargain. He could already imagine the priest rejoicing over the double blessing—the tapestry, and the return of a true penitent (a strictly temporary one) after a long absence from the fold.

But it was not to be. "That's just the kind of insane scheme I would expect from a Richier," Claude had said. "We don't want any cinema, thank you very much. Just get the rotten thing back—anonymously."

Jean reluctantly decided to sacrifice the *grand guignol*. But Xavier, in a state of fury, had one last, bitter trick up his sleeve: a way to hit back—though only a small blow—and also to assuage the Richier pride. Sacrificing the finest piece in his collection was an agony. Claude Saudeville followed Xavier's instructions to the letter. "You put your own name and address here," the functionary at the station had explained. Saudeville nodded. Using a red ink felt-tipped pen he wrote in large block capitals next to "Sender": FROM JACQUES DUPONT—HISTORIC MONUMENTS DEPT: THE LOUVRE.

A few days later Commissaire Chevalier heard the news by telephone from a puzzled police inspector in Le Mans, who wanted to know what was going on. *Le Patron* did not know exactly, but all the same he found it very funny. Monsieur Dupont, on the other hand, did not. He viewed the whole thing as a joke in the worst possible taste.

CHAPTER XVII

The Obsession with Faïence

It was a hot afternoon at the end of May, 1964, and Xavier
Richier was examining the seventeenth-century tapestry in the
Museum of St. Vaast at Arras, the capital of the Pas-de-Calais
fifteen miles from Liévin. Xavier had chosen to adopt what he
liked to think of as his international art expert *persona*. So he
had on neither the old gabardine mackintosh, nor the deplorable
jacket which he took to be good enough for his patients. The
mac was carried, folded up, on his arm. Apart from this, the
doctor was a resplendent figure in his lightweight suit of raw
silk and flowing tie—his Paris uniform. Anyone who had
observed him, and someone did, would have noticed that he
seemed in an emotional state. The wonderful tapestry had gone
back to Le Mans; fear had finally triumphed over his possessive
instinct. Now every time he as much as saw some reference to a
tapestry in one of his catalogues, or noticed the blank patch on
the wall where his Le Mans St. Gervais had hung for two years
he was overtaken by despair.

The Arras tapestries, Xavier thought, were inferior—later in
the afternoon he indiscreetly lectured the curator's assistant on
the subject, and even said that he himself possessed a far finer
mediaeval example than anything in Arras. In the same conversation—Xavier almost seemed to be taking risks deliberately
—he attacked the Arras Museum authorities and the Beaux
Arts section of the Historic Monuments Department, his *bête*

noire at this period, for the insensitive way they had restored a set of eighteenth-century chairs. In this instance he had some right on his side for the chairs had been regilded *au ripolin*—that is, by a heavy paint process, which has the effect of blunting the carving. Xavier completed his lecture with a few words about faïence, his newest interest.

After ten minutes the irritated official managed to detach himself from this self-opinionated visitor who had chosen to tell him his own business at such tedious length. His annoyance was increased by the coincidence of a visit from the R.T.F., the French counterpart of the B.B.C., who had arrived that afternoon at Arras to film a special exhibition of seventeenth- and eighteenth-century drawings of which the museum was very proud. Everything was chaotic with technicians shouting at each other, and submerging the place in electric cables, arc-lights and cameras. The official found the programme producer and walked off with him.

But Xavier revenged himself swiftly; it was a perfect opportunity. Apart from the R.T.F., the museum was full of milling tourists. He swooped on a side table which was used to display one of the museum's best small pieces, a *jardinière* in Marseilles faïence showing a *fête champêtre* scene in delicate greens and white. Xavier put it under his arm and left the building; no one challenged, or even noticed him. He walked to the yellow Dauphine parked in the rue de la Madeleine and carefully wrapping his new acquisition in tissue paper, stowed it in the boot.

It was an exquisite piece, and consoled him to some extent for the loss of the tapestry. After a remarkable Salle Drouot sale of faïence six months before, this art form had become his new obsession, and he had studied intensively to make himself an authority. He had read all available books and catalogues, and visited a score of museums with distinguished faïence on display. He was also able to make some clandestine researches into one of the finest private collections in Europe: at Drouot he had been fortunate enough to meet another enthusiast who had visited the Château des Boulayes on one of its extremely rare "open days" when members of a learned society were allowed to look round the house.

The doctor was determined that Claude's defection, as he regarded it, was not going to hold him back. If he had to change his approach and actually do the raids himself, then so be it. He hadn't done so badly at the Musée St. Vaast. On impulse he now pointed the car north-west towards Aire-sur-la-Lys; he would have another look at the Boeseghem faïence, which he had promised himself. A quiet Sunday afternoon would probably be best for the actual raid; today he could reconnoitre the Cathedral of St. Pierre in Aire, and even have a look at the Virgin in Thiennes at the same time. Known as Notre Dame de Joyel, it was a statue which he was determined would eventually be in his private rooms in Liévin, where he could clean and restore it. Meanwhile he pondered cheerfully on the possibilities at St. Pierre. It would serve as a curtain-raiser to the new *coup* he was planning—at the Château des Boulayes.

The Château des Boulayes is one of the most beautiful eighteenth-century houses in Europe. It is one of the twenty or so finest examples of the simple rectangle design, and succeeds so perfectly because of the flawless rhythm of its flat Corinthian pillars, set against the absolutely straight entrance drive, framed by a line of beeches roughly a mile long. The effect is at once monumental, and yet light and graceful. Unfortunately it is not open to the public, for Boulayes seen on a summer's evening produces one of the most haunting images in French architecture.

Les Boulayes is in the Seine-et-Oise department just twenty-four miles east of Paris, standing back from N4, the Nancy Road. The nearest village is Touran-en-Brie, five minutes' drive away. Like so many eighteenth-century châteaux, Les Boulayes was rebuilt and redesigned (in 1785, by the Prix de Rome winner, Girardin) on a site where two earlier châteaux had stood. It was, at this time, owned by a certain Claude Bellanger, who apart from being a Colonel of the Royal Guards, has acquired a minute *niche* in history because of his mysterious relationship with Madame Jeanne du Barry.

The Colonel was for many years her most trusted *confidant*, but he was a singularly ineffective man, dogged by failure. The Château des Boulayes was his only solid achievement. His

wealth came from Madame du Barry, who rewarded him generously for the series of confidential missions he performed for
her. Unfortunately, his most important assignment on Madame
du Barry's behalf turned into a fiasco. Despatched to England,
in order to pursue (and presumably liquidate) a certain Theve-
not de Morande, author of a libellous, and doubtless accurate,
account of Louis XV's sexual escapades at Versailles and elsewhere, Colonel Bellanger managed somehow to run aground
in the Thames. He returned to France to tell how he had
escaped drowning by a hair's breadth (and, incidentally, completely failed to find his man). A lesser woman might have taken
it badly but Jeanne du Barry behaved with magnaminity; she
even found Bellanger an extremely beautiful wife, a natural
daughter of Louis XV. In the usual manner she had been
equipped with both a splendid dowry and a *de jure* father.
Colonel Bellanger hoped to found a great dynasty, and built
Les Boulayes for his bride. But he was unlucky, as usual, and
the new Madame Bellanger proved to have inherited too many
characteristics from her parents to adapt contentedly to a sedate,
if elegant, domesticity. Eventually, a liaison with the Prince de
Conti, the most outrageously public of an impressive series of
infidelities, was too much even for the long-suffering Colonel.
The couple separated. Came the Revolution and Bellanger
emigrated hurriedly—and alone.

The château was naturally confiscated and then passed
through the hands of numerous owners, including the Duc de
Bourbon. It now belongs to John and Fanny Bouboulis (her
father bought it in 1909) who have gradually restored Les
Boulayes since the war, during which it was successively and
destructively occupied by, in turn, the German and U.S.
armies; repatriated French prisoners of war; orphan children
and, finally, nearly 300 Jewish displaced refugees from
Auschwitz. By the summer of 1964 the house, surrounded by a
moat and 2,500 acres of park and farmland, where Louis XVI
had hunted, was once again in perfect condition. And it became
the home of the family's art treasures, including their remarkable collection of faïence. That is, until the afternoon of June
23rd, 1964—two days after Xavier Richier's tour of churches in
the Pas-de-Calais. The theft combined simplicity, nerve and

first-class information. The Bouboulis family were away: Marie, the maid, was ironing in the linen room on the first floor, and downstairs three estate employees were repainting the kitchen. It was a hot day, and the painters worked sporadically, due to Beauty, the Bouboulis' sealyham, who was exploring the paint, and to their own frequent need to refresh and relieve themselves.

The thief arrived by a lane which curls round the back of the château from the Nancy road. There is a dense wood of larch, poplars and pines, penetrated by narrow firebreaks. He parked the car, and moved cautiously up to the outhouses behind the château. Once the painters in the kitchen took a break, it was simply a matter of crossing thirty yards of cobbles unobserved. He went through the big, airy kitchen and into a curiously-furnished room known as the *salle-de-chasse* (a kind of gun-room) filled with club chairs, *fauteuils*, a large oil painting of dead game, and an exceptional Chinese painted screen.

The noise he made attracted the attention of Marie in the linen-room, who assumed that the painters must be invading the family's section of the house, and came downstairs with the intention of driving them off. She bustled into the *salle-de-chasse* — but saw no one. At this moment, the thief was hiding behind the Chinese screen. The maid smelt smoke in the air, and resolved to tell the painters, as soon as she could find them, that she knew they had been in the room. (It was only afterwards that the stub of the intruder's cigarette was found behind the screen.)

When she had gone upstairs again, the thief walked through into the main entrance hall, turned left and entered the dining-room which leads off the hall. The first thing he did was lock the connecting door between the dining-room and the kitchen. This is, in fact, only the western room in a suite of three, all eighteen feet high, and joined by interconnecting doors, looking out through full-length windows over the terraces to the woods behind the house.

The thief continued into the main salon. His target was the Louis XVI *vitrine*, or display cabinet, just inside the connecting door, which contains the collection of *bleu-de-chine* porcelain built up by Fanny Bouboulis' father. This was locked: the key

141

was one of a bunch of ten hidden in a secret drawer in a small Louis XVI lady's writing-desk, next to the vitrine. The thief took the key, opened the cabinet, and removed from the twelve items on display four of the most distinguished.

In another cabinet in the same room there was a unique set of seventeen dinner plates of Marseilles faïence: this is the attractively thick, brightly decorated clay china which was general in Europe until porcelain appeared in the middle of the eighteenth century. Marseilles faïence, which is rare, is usually distinguished by a golden arrow mark on the back; very occasionally there is a double golden arrow, and this was the case with this set. It was almost perfect, but one plate had been broken and expertly, undetectably mended. The thief took the sixteen perfect plates. Now he went briefly into a small bedroom beside the dining-room, sometimes used by John Bouboulis. Here, he took some 1000-franc notes from a red leather box, and on his way back through the dining-room he stuffed all the solid silver spoons and forks into his pockets. But then he must have panicked: he needed to take the knives to get the full value of the Louis XVI cutlery. Such a set is worth £30,000 complete, but only £600 incomplete.

He was in enough of a hurry going down the firebreak on his departure to drop three forks and a spoon in the grass. This was Thursday night. The theft was not discovered until next evening, when Marie began to prepare the table for the family's Friday evening arrival from Paris. She found the dining-room locked, and no key. When with some difficulty she had let herself in at the french windows. She laid the knives—and found no spoons or forks. At that moment, the Bouboulis arrived. Johnny Bouboulis phoned the police at Tournan-en-Brie, two miles away.

Subsequently the dubious organisation of the French police system began to show itself. It was two hours later that the police car arrived. After another two hours the *flics* completed their search, apparently somewhat dispirited at the lack of gun-play. The family, who had worked out the extent of their losses, sat the pair down in the dining-room and gave them a large drink. Then they left promising to return the day after with reinforcements. The police did not, however, reappear until Monday.

Presumably they did not quite realise that they were dealing with a £15,000 robbery. When they came back there was a Commissaire de Police from Nancy with them, who gave a more professional tone to the investigation by taking down the names and addresses of past employees. But they did not fingerprint the house, and the search of the grounds was only just good enough to uncover the silver which the thief had dropped.

CHAPTER XVIII

The Aesthetic Thief

Alone among the exotic, sexy throng on the ground floor of the Café Floré, Claude Mabilotte drank Scotch in doubles—he might as well spend Jean's money while he could—and despaired. What was there ahead? The rest of his sentence for Neuville, and then perhaps a yet longer sentence on top, if that bastard Chevalier ever got on to the Richiers. He ordered another drink, then another. From time to time men would smile at him invitingly but he ignored them.

He stayed an hour, while the crowd formed and reformed, fixing dinner appointments and assignations, eyeing each overtly, assessing the prospects.

Eventually Claude got up, supporting himself on the green table-top, determined to escape the heat and noise. Indeed, determined to escape everything. He was going home to kill himself.

But Claude was badly informed on suicide techniques. He swallowed forty aspirins, only enough to make himself wretchedly sick for two days. On the morning of the third, he woke up, felt better, and decided the time had come to clear out of Paris. Accordingly, he packed, collected the red Fiat from the garage, called on his lawyer, and then visited his doctor.

That afternoon, to their chagrin, the G.R.B. found themselves tapping a call from Mabilotte to their own headquarters.

He was humble, but determined. Could he please have permission to make the prescribed regular probation reports to the Commissariat of Police in Marseilles, instead of Paris. He was armed with a medical certificate saying he required convalescence in the south.

Chevalier could have delayed such a move, but he decided to assent, even though Claude's departure would frustrate his stratagem, at least temporarily. Le Bruchec came from Corsica, had relations in Marseilles, and for a few days was hopeful of continuing his surveillance in the *Midi*. Chevalier vetoed the idea, and simply warned his Marseilles colleagues to keep a watch on Claude. But he thought the trail had gone cold.

Chevalier was right, until September when le Bruchec's long *filature* of Claude Mabilotte was justified many times over. A routine check on Mabilotte's phone calls, just before he returned to Pontoise to stand trial for the Neuville affair, produced a report that was eventually to clinch the affair. At the time, however, neither le Bruchec nor anyone else thought it of any particular importance.

So the summer months produced nothing, except a brief orientation to the south and south-west. During this time the coincidence of three extremely important thefts of faïence in under four weeks (at the end of May, on June 2nd, and June 23rd), might have given Chevalier a strong hint that his long-cherished *Gentleman Cambrioleur* had finally tired of the eighteenth-century *ébenistes* and was collecting something new. As Jacques Dupont had valuably pointed out, the thieves' taste had shown a consistent development. But the faïence thefts made little impact—a long study of furniture and ecclesiastical art thefts had deflected Chevalier's interest from anything else, particularly pottery. But there was a much more important reason. The three faïence reports were lost in a deluge of theft notifications which for a period during the summer flowed into the Faubourg St. Honoré office almost daily.

They all seemed to have taken place in western and south-western France, and, though they occasionally involved private houses (always uninhabited ones), the major concentration involved museums and, above all, cathedrals and churches.

The objects stolen varied from trifles to pieces of great importance like the celebrated Christ of Corbières, a wonderful mediaeval statue which disappeared in August from the church near Perpignan where it had stood for four centuries. This piece had been valued at nearly £40,000, an extremely conservative estimate, and it was also classified as part of the national patrimony.

The G.R.B. was deeply alarmed; it sounded too much like Laval and Le Mans all over again—these were the kind of thefts that carried infuriated Ministerial memoranda in their wake, sometimes signed by the great André Malraux himself.

Within days of the Perpignan report Chevalier received a copy of yet another, a massive document from Interpol. It originally had been compiled by the Spanish police working with Dr. Xavier da Salas, Director-Designate of the Prado Museum in Madrid. At first glance it read like an inventory of half the museums and churches in northern Spain. In due course, further lists arrived from Bordeaux, La Rochelle, Nantes, Tours and Châteauroux. The last name produced a new train of thought; Châteauroux, before de Gaulle's withdrawal from N.A.T.O., was the site of one of the most important U.S. Air Force bases in France, and from time to time had been under suspicion as the centre of large-scale illegal transportation of one kind and another. The most notorious case was that of a former U.S.A.F. public information Major who had settled in the area after retirement. He had been arrested for massive imports and exports of heroin, using scheduled U.S.A.F. flights between Rhein-Main, Châteauroux, and various bases all over the United States.

If they have a pass, service personnel (with their luggage) can hitch rides easily enough on transport flights with empty places. A kit-bag and a leave pass open the door to the simplest, fastest and most foolproof method of shifting a statuette, or a mediaeval tapestry, from a cathedral in the French countryside to Fifth Avenue, or Rio.

The police had long been puzzling over how so many objects had managed to disappear altogether. There was remarkably little evidence of stolen antiques being resold through the French trade, legitimate or unscrupulous. Perhaps the whole gang had moved, Chevalier thought—to the south-west and Spain.

The Commissaire's first reaction to the report of the Corbères theft had been to ask the Marseilles police where Claude Mabilotte had been at the time. They had been able to establish beyond any doubt that he had been convalescing at Cassis, near Marseilles—to be precise in a harbour bar called the Café de la Marine, a good ten hours' drive from the church in the lower Pyrénées.

The Châteauroux trail turned out to be entirely misleading. Many of the police hypotheses were correct; Xavier and Jean Richier *were* on holiday, they had taken a luxurious villa near Tunis, but Xavier, mollified by his satisfactory run with faïence, was not thinking about art thefts. Jean, too, was concentrating on relaxation.

It was the worst possible luck for the police that the man responsible for the thefts in Spain, south-western, and western central France, should have been in so many ways similar to Xavier Richier, though the two were not even aware of each other's existence.

Alain Michel, then twenty-six, had hardly had time to mature as a connoisseur, but he had already acquired a very extensive collection, the main concentration being on mediaeval ecclesiastical art, a field Xavier himself had always collected. Michel's own collection, much larger though less valuable than the doctor's, revealed knowledge, taste and obsessional interest. And in common with Xavier's, it had yet another distinguishing feature. Michel had acquired it without spending a centime.

Alain Michel had been born and brought up in Poitiers, a beautiful and historic town, but he found it just as provincial as Xavier did Liévin. The two men shared many reactions, and even obsessions. In the first place Michel, like Richier, *looked* odd. His lank hair was shoulder length and Beatle-style (in Poitiers they say patriotically "à la Jeanne d'Arc"), at a time when all respectable Frenchmen insisted on short haircuts; only tramps and major exhibitionists had got around to the long look. Unlike Richier, Michel went out of his way to shock and annoy. He paraded his homosexuality and made no secret of the fact that he regarded Poitiers society, revolving as it does round commerce and the ancient University, as philistine and dreary. Michel reckoned he was the only sophisticate in a *petit-bourgeois* world. There was no one to sympathise or share his intellectual passions; like the doctor, he adopted antiques as an escape.

"It's been my recurrent dream ever since I was a child to possess a perfect, imaginary museum of my own," Michel confided to his highly able lawyer, Maître Henri-Paul Moinet. "That's why I stole so much—all I wanted was to create an ambience around me that was perfectly beautiful." And with this idea as his justification he had started in 1963 to steal odd objects from museums and churches; a year later Michel was completely dedicated to what he saw as the most exciting—and rewarding—game anyone had ever thought up. He managed to acquire a ramshackle country cottage at Migné-Auxances, a hamlet ten miles out of Poitiers and, by coincidence, not far from the Benedictine Monastery of Liguge, specialising in hand-made Limoges pottery, where Xavier Richier sometimes used to say he was going to retire.

Michel set to work to turn his new cottage into a museum, and a year later it contained over 2,500 separate items, all of them stolen. Like Xavier he often sat up all night admiring a new acquisition. He was also in the habit of making one-day *tours d'horizon*, taking down elaborate notes and sketches for future "collecting" itineraries. Michel's exercise books were filled with meticulous observations: what time the Curator at La Rochelle Museum took his pre-lunch aperitif, and the width of the porticos at a Romanesque church where he had designs on a particularly grandiose piece of statuary. But by no means all Michel's numerous thefts were premeditated. If he saw something he liked, and thought he had a chance of getting away with, he would remove it on the spot.

He worked almost entirely on the "shop-lifting" principle, and seldom broke in anywhere. In general it wasn't necessary. The churches and museums he visited were badly protected and those entrusted with the objects they contained rarely knew or cared anything about them.

This indifference meant that days or even weeks frequently elapsed between a theft and the time it was reported. Sometimes

no one noticed the loss at all, and many objects were later returned to owners who were surprised to learn that they had ever
been removed.

The cottage was soon bulging with a magpie collection of
furniture, statues, *bibelots* of all kinds, vast antique mirrors,
and purloined velvet draperies, usually in red. Among many
objects stolen from churches in Poitiers itself were innumerable
candelabra and a complete set of Bishop's ceremonial vestments,
which Michel liked to wear when conducting boy-friends round
his museum.

Most of the thefts took place on Sundays, or in the evenings,
for the rest of Michel's time was occupied working in his parents' photography business—the Michels own a shop in Poitiers,
dealing mainly with family groups and new babies. It was not
the kind of work which gave Michel much opportunity to realise
his considerable artistic talents (he was an excellent photographer of antiques, and an accomplished draughtsman).

But he was able to make use of his days off, and he devoted
his annual holidays exclusively to theft. The reports from Interpol were the result of a fortnight's trip he had taken to Spain.
He had gone to a good deal of trouble to set up the operation;
a Professor at Poitiers University, who was impressed by Michel's
knowledge of antiques, had even been persuaded to provide
letters of introduction to the curators of a number of important
Spanish museums. After ten days Michel's borrowed Deux-
Cheveaux van was so heavily loaded with plundered items that
he had trouble getting through the Pyrénées on the way back.
At the border checkpoint Customs Officials naturally wanted
to know what was weighing the old car down on its springs. The
exchange which followed was an ideal example of the situation
when the art thief meets the small bureaucrat. If Michel had
been carrying worthless souvenirs, goatskins of wine, indeed
virtually anything that seemed bright and new, he would have
had a difficult forty minutes, and a bill at the end.

As it was mediaeval crucifixes, including an unwieldy eight
foot bronze Christ from a church in Catalonia, polychrome Virgins, pictures, and other items of such quality and variety that
Xavier da Salas from the Prado Museum later spent three complete days compiling an inventory of them, the Customs simply

told Michel he must be mad to carry that kind of junk around, and waved him through without charge. Michel then stopped overnight at Corbères, to visit the famous church. When he set off on the last lap of the journey home he had another parcel, tied this time on the roof of the car as there was no more space inside.

The amazing thing is that he was able to steal so effectively, simply by going through the front door, selecting what he wanted (always in broad daylight), and then carrying it out the way he had come. Bihn had used the same approach when removing the sixteenth-century tapestry from the Basilica d'Avesnières at Laval, but Bihn was a respectable figure in his well-cut dark suit, and he had gone to the trouble of backing this up with a story about being from the Beaux Arts (a variation on his usual line of being a restorer on business). Michel, with the flowing hair, jeans, and dusty battle-dress jacket, was the kind of figure officials of all kinds suspect on sight.

Michel never sold anything. He took things because he wanted them, and the idea of stealing for profit, according to his neurotic logic, would have been not only immoral, but mad. It is clear that Xavier Richier began in the same spirit, and by a curious, circular progression seems at the very end of his career to have arrived back where he started—it had become so painful to lose the things he had stolen, or, more usually, had stolen for him, that he was reluctant ever to sell them.

If Michel had continued (he was arrested about two and a half years after his first theft), would he too have reached the point of selling his objects? It is unlikely, judging from his previous history, and some clues to his unusual psychology which emerged from explanations during his trial.

For Michel, it seemed necessary to steal objects in order to enjoy them—the more reckless the risk involved, the happier he was, and the more precious the new addition to his collection. There was probably an element of masochism present. He took such wild chances that had it not been for the consistent myopia and indifference of the people he stole from, he must surely have been caught repeatedly. At the end of his career, Michel seems to have stolen like those gamblers who play to lose.

As the Head Waiter of the Café de la Paix, which passes for the social centre of Poitiers, remarked shortly after Michel's arrest: "How could any sane man have taken the cathedral affair seriously? Naturally, I thought it was a drunk's fairy story." In fact, it was one of Michel's more carefully planned jobs. The idea first came to him when he discovered a set of discarded and worthless Napoleon III chandeliers in the basement of Poitiers Town Hall. He removed the lustres from the chandeliers and took them to his cottage, but not because he liked them. They were strictly a short-term investment.

In January 1964 he moved them into a room, seldom used and next to the vestry, east of the chancel in the Cathedral of St. Peter in Poitiers. Architecturally the Gothic Cathédral St. Pierre is not in the same class as its Romanesque Gothic neighbour, Notre Dame la Grande, but it is a fine building, and one where Alain Michel was known and accepted. He helped organise their annual pageant, taking advantage of the occasions to steal formal vestments for use in his fantasy life at Migné-Auxances.

Perhaps the masterpieces of St. Peter are the chandeliers, dating from the sixteenth century, classically constructed, exquisitely balanced, light and airy. Michel wanted them, and worked for ten nights to get them. He hid every evening in a confessional, until the great doors were locked at six o'clock. He then emerged and carried an extendable maintenance ladder, thirty feet long, to the centre of the church to reach the chandeliers. Working only by torchlight, he not only dismembered four of the chandeliers, a piece at a time, but also remade them using his store of lustres from the Napoleon III chandeliers at the Town Hall. Finally, Michel installed the cathedral chandeliers so that they extended the length of his drawing-room, already lined with tall, *rococo* mirrors, the origins of which have never been established. Michel talked illuminatingly about this operation to Maître Moinet before the trial.

"I was terrified there alone in the dark every night—but when it was over and I had them home I felt liberated. I went around as if I was drunk all the time."

It sounds like an adolescent's description of first love, and it can hardly be a coincidence that so many of the men who have been arrested over the last few years for art thefts have been immature personalities, frequently homosexual, and usually unsuccessful—except at stealing, and even then their luck is not inexhaustible. Like Xavier, the doctor who was nervous even of driving a car, and yet found from somewhere the audacity to walk into the Arras Museum, talk to an official, pick up a piece of faïence he fancied, and march out with it under his arm, Michel was looking for adventure as well as escapism.

It is quite clear that for him the "Affair of the Cathedral" was an apogee; after that anything else could only be anti-climax. He may not have been consciously aware that he was trying to get himself arrested, but there is no other explanation of his behaviour.

Poitiers possesses one of the oldest universities in France. The students' café in the Place du Maréchal Leclerc, called of course the Café de la Paix, is a vast Edwardian institution with green leather *banquettes*, which for want of anywhere more exciting is the traditional meeting place of Poitiers' young society. Michel was well known there.

He was regarded as the best teller of tall stories in the city. After the St. Pierre *coup* he must at different times have explained what he had done to twenty different people. For some time he had talked openly about thefts from museums and churches. No one had believed him; again no one took any notice of the new story. Apart from its intrinsic unlikeliness, it was inconceivable that if someone had changed over the chandeliers, the cathedral authorities would not have taken action. The truth was more incredible; they simply didn't notice.

In the end Michel managed to get himself caught, which perhaps gave him some satisfaction—at least his chandelier story was believed.

He took a friend to a museum at La Rochelle and stole a ring from a small cabinet under the eyes of the female curator. She noticed nothing at the time but then, just before going home for the night, saw that there was a blank space. She telephoned the police and described Michel, an easy subject. There was no room for doubt because, such is the appeal of provincial museums, he and his friend had been the only visitors all day. The hairy photographer was arrested at his favourite table in the Café de la Paix at the aperitif hour. He was actually wearing the ring when the police arrived. He went with them quite contentedly, it seemed, and after they had visited Migné-Auxances and returned astounded at what they had found, he helped them to compile an inventory and trace owners. They did not succeed in returning all the goods because at some points Michel's memory failed him. And, as with the St. Pierre chandeliers, no reports of a good proportion of the thefts had ever been made.

From the psychiatric point of view, Michel's defence was straightforward—an unbalanced, unhappy personality with family and sexual problems, had tried to find emotional release in obsessional theft. The defence (very skilfully) presented their case as if Michel was so sick that there could be no question of free will. He, himself, was simpler, and extremely honest.

"I wanted beautiful things, so I took them. The owners did not care one way or the other, so what harm was I doing? I didn't hurt anyone."

The prosecution were not legally persuaded by the excuse, but they were merciful enough to see that Michel was in the grip of a kind of mania. They also saw that he had never acted for commercial ends. One of the policemen who had arrested him, and had also investigated his earlier career, told the court that when as an adolescent he had been apprenticed to a photographer at La Rochelle, he had only been prepared to accept his wages under persuasion. Sometimes he lived for a week without spending fifty centimes. As a senior policeman said: "Personally, he was the complete aesthete. And as a criminal, the purest of pure amateurs."

In May 1965, Michel was sentenced to two years' imprisonment, which was mild. The saddest fact of the whole affair was that his respectable family promptly refused to have anything to do with him—even to visit him in prison. Michel was probably lucky to have been caught. In time, his compulsion might have driven him to more involved self-justifications, less forgiveable kinds of theft, and perhaps even to violence. As it was, unlike Xavier Richier, he had succeeded in preserving his innocence.

There was a postscript to the story.

When they were first informed of the arrest, the St. Pierre dignitaries simply refused to believe that anything had happened to the chandeliers. Very reluctantly, they were convinced. They then found themselves with a problem—how were they going to restore their desecrated chandeliers? The decision caused them much anguish and several months after the arrest, their original lustres, retrieved from Michel's cottage, were still sitting in the same room next to the vestry (though now bearing the Judge of Instruction's label) where Michel had stowed substitutes nearly a year before.

And Michel, a model prisoner, guessed what was happening. He asked permission to send a message to the cathedral. It was entirely without sarcasm and perfectly expressed his naïvety, the child-like unfallen quality which had typified his behaviour from the beginning.

"I'd be happy to restore the chandeliers for the Fathers if they would let me. I expect it will be hard to find anyone else who is interested enough, and it would be tragic to make a mess of the job."

The cathedral dignitaries huffily declined even to reply.

Meanwhile the precious lustres were acquiring an ever deeper coating of vestry dust.

CHAPTER XIX

"Break-through"

To the police Michel was guilty of a greater crime; his 2,000 felonies had led them into false hypotheses which had confused their major investigation for several months. But René Chevalier had a break-through in the autumn—a tapped telephone conversation from Claude Mabilotte (still under surveillance by le Bruchec). It added a new name to their list of Mabilotte's contacts; a young decorator, Jean Richier.

Or it seemed new until Louis Raton laboriously checked back through the case dossier and happened on the report from a Judge of Instruction, M Villa du Parc, who had been called in at the beginning of 1963 to provide a supplementary inquest, or *"instruction"* on the château thefts. Villa du Parc had done a thorough job, though his results had been inconclusive. In the course of checking the sixteen *fauteuils* stolen from Villarceaux in August, 1963, he had called at the Richier flat in Place Léon-Blum. This was because someone in the Salle Drouot vaguely remembered that Jean Richier had been trying to sell a pair of Louis XV chairs, similar to those from the Duc de Villefranche's château. Villa du Parc did not find these chairs at Jean's home —they had long gone. But he did notice a pair of Louis XVI transitional chairs. These were shown to the Villarceaux *régisseur*, whose unlikely name was Charles Boyer, and he said that he had never seen them before in his life.

In fact, the chairs were among those stolen by Huré and Mabi-

lotte from the Château de Ménars that January. It had been a
bad fortnight for Jean Richier but in the end he got his
(Ménars) *fauteuils* back again with a note from the magistrates
exonerating him from all suspicion, and thanking him for his
co-operation.

Villa du Parc's near-miss did have one important by-product;
the name Jean Richier received a minor mention in his exhaustive and thoroughly professional report.

Joseph le Bruchec and Louis Raton were by now prepared
to try any approach and they mentioned Jean's name to everyone they met in the dealers' *milieu* during the next few days.
Among other people, they visited Maurice Giffard, a very correct connoisseur who runs a shop called Jeanne Fillon at 29, rue
Jacob and 23, rue Bonaparte—it straddles the intersection of
the two streets. M. Giffard was unwilling to say anything at all,
but the police assured him it was nothing important—"entirely
for the record". He believed them. So he said that Jean was a
decorator who had often bought *art nouveau* pieces for the
boutique, though not in recent months. He mentioned two
other things in passing, both kindly intended; he wanted the
police to be convinced of Jean's impeccable respectability.

The young decorator, Giffard said, came from an excellent
family. He had a wealthy brother, a doctor from somewhere in
the north, who often visited Paris as he was a quite important
collector of classical furniture, and often attended big sales at
Drouot. This was the unfortunate legacy of a Saturday morning
Xavier had spent showing off in the boutique. Giffard added
another point; Jean was the protégé of a most important *Gaul-
list* official, who had known the family since Jean was a child.
(This was entirely true, but as the official in question was in
no way connected with the shady side of Jean's life he will remain anonymous.) The police continued their inquiries elsewhere. They learned nothing against Jean at a shop called
A.B.C. in the rue Mazarin where he had worked so long.
Madame Levy said that Jean was totally honest. A few hundred
words on him were added to the hundreds of thousands already
filed at 257, rue du Faubourg St. Honoré, under the heading
"Château Gang".

It was nevertheless the most important break-through for the

police since Mabilotte and Huré had made the foolish decision
to raid the Château de Neuville, independent of the Richiers
and Bihn. It meant that Jean had twice been noted in connection with the affair. The police had no idea of the importance
of these entries. But they were crucial; a piece in the puzzle of
the Château Gang, the one marked "Richier", was there, ready
to be slotted into the central place when the right moment came.

When Jean, who was just back from Tunis, heard that two
flics had been asking questions about him he immediately
panicked. He rang Xavier saying they must emigrate—and was
told magisterially not to be an idiot.

In terror, and needing a friend, Jean arrived one morning at
the end of September, 1964, at the first class antique shop owned
by his friend and former *patron*, Jean-Pierre Hagnauer. Hagnauer was pleased, and slightly surprised, to see him. Only the
previous evening Hagnauer's wife had wondered: "Why don't
we see Jean any more?" Two years before he had been working
in the shop virtually every day, but for over six months there
had been no sign of him. Her husband replied that according
to trade gossip Jean had made a break-through as a decorator;
after years of near-poverty he was apparently rich. On the last
occasion he had appeared in the rue de Seine he had boasted of
the wonderful furniture he had acquired: "They wouldn't do
for you though," he had added.

The Hagnauers are kind people and Jean-Pierre had hoped
their former protégé would pass the morning recounting other
triumphs. But surprisingly he became near-hysterical, repeating
again and again that he must get out of the antiques business
altogether.

"I couldn't understand him at all, particularly as he seemed
at last to have won a serious reputation. It didn't make sense. I
gave him a cup of coffee and he calmed down." Hagnauer is a
shrewd man who knew a lot about Jean, and he was puzzled.

"I wondered what kind of a mess the boy had got himself into.
I was sure he wasn't telling the truth when he said the antiques
business was corrupt, and so on. He was obviously using this as
an excuse to let off steam about something else that was bother-
ing him. I'd always been aware he was homosexual. I guessed
his lover had left him. Then I wondered whether he was being

blackmailed—poor old Jean started crying. I asked if he needed any money."

Jean said money was no problem. In earlier days he had borrowed from Hagnauer incessantly, and never once failed to pay him back. Like Xavier he was straight with his friends. He had also borrowed from his doctor, Boris Ossipovsky, a skin specialist in the rue de Villiers, who had long been treating him for nervous allergies. Ossipovsky was repaid, and was also sold several important items of stolen furniture at knock-down prices (which after Jean's arrest the police decided had been bought in good faith). They also showed a lot of interest in a faïence *potiche de Chine* which the doctor had received as an Easter present from his devoted patient in 1963.

"Jean kept insisting he was finished with antiques and talked of getting a job in an architect's office," Hagnauer went on: "It sounded sensible in a way as he had some talent for drawing. I said I'd keep a look out for anything, but I didn't take it too seriously. Frankly, it sounded simply like a *projet d'évasion* pulled out of the air on impulse—I think he was obsessed by a need to escape. He was scared stiff, poor old lad."

Hagnauer's assessment was very acute and Jean virtually disappeared during the early winter. Before Christmas he was in Tunis again and when the Hagnauers next saw him, in January, 1965, he seemed more relaxed.

The architecture project was never mentioned again. And he kept as far away from art thefts, and his erstwhile colleagues, as possible. There was nothing the police could fasten on him, particularly as André Huré had been in prison all the time, and Claude Mabilotte, his "provisional liberty for health reasons" expired, had rejoined his old colleague in prison at Pontoise. It was a quiet winter for château robberies.

Xavier went to Tunis at Christmas and returned in high good humour with numerous crates of oranges which he distributed generously to friends, and local children, whom he had always found easier to deal with than their parents.

He flew off again for North Africa in March—"the weather in Liévin is a negation of life, I must have sun to resuscitate me," he told Dr. Westeel grandly before departure. The locum, paid a pittance as Xavier's assistant, doing most of the work, and with his two children scarcely able to afford a week's holiday at Trouville, felt piqued. Xavier was treating his responsibility to the miners in an increasingly cavalier way, and it was widely predicted that he would soon resign—or be fired. In Paris, Jean was once again leading a gay social life but staying honest. He had been frightened too badly to embark on fresh projects.

Solidly, doggedly, in the course of that winter, the G.R.B. had managed to track down something like twenty different stolen objects. A picture, stolen three years earlier, was found at Marcel Bihn's on the Quai Malaquais. The police did a routine check on the adventurous former O.A.S. man, which proved that his three closest associates had been André Huré, Claude Mabilotte and—Jean Richier, even though Jean had been around rarely of late, and the other two had been out of circulation altogether.

Chevalier immediately ordered a check on this last name, which he very faintly remembered. The G.R.B. discovered their dossier from the previous September—a contact of Claude Mabilotte, it said. There remained a note of Villa du Parc's abortive discovery of the wrong chairs, and also the report of one vaguely suspicious telephone conversation between Jean and Mabilotte. This meant little; they had a list of roughly thirty calls from Mabilotte to different people, apparently without significance. But the doctor brother in the north interested Chevalier. He asked Inspector Louis Raton to try and follow it up.

The investigation had been dragging for months. Suddenly it began to move at a gallop, like a joke sequence in an avantgarde film. Le Bruchec obtained a list of customers from the account book (the public one) at the Quai Malaquais, despite Marcel's objections, first bland, and then furious. The first calls were blanks. Then in the course of one afternoon on March 28th, 1965, le Bruchec in turn visited two apartments, both newly and expensively redecorated. Both contained Boulard *fauteuils* which the burly inspector thought were suspicious. He started to check at once; it took him until dawn. He juggled with innumerable photographs, cross-checking inventory after inventory; a painful process as le Bruchec found paperwork anathema. At last, as the first of the cleaners collected their pails in the hallway, the former Murder Squad detective, so far away from his preferred beat, clambered into the G.R.B.'s monstrous Edwardian wrought-iron lift, and let himself out in front of the cold façade of St. Philippe du Roule. There was no doubt; the *fauteuils* had been stolen. Their descriptions were buried among lists of furniture missing since a theft three years before.

At eight a.m. he was in a coin box, ringing the apartment owners; they were respectable, rather wealthy men, one a dentist, the other a former advocate at the Algerian bar in Oran, now in retirement. They told precisely the same story. Le Bruchec was convinced that they had acquired their furniture in good faith.

"Did you buy the Boulard *fauteuils* from Marcel Bihn, M'sieur?"

"The Boulards? Oh, no, they were recommended and purchased by the decorator. He did an excellent job. To be frank, I thought the chairs were a bargain."

"The decorator's name?" They both said Jean Richier.

It was nine-fifteen when Louis Raton and le Bruchec arrived outside the heavy oak, double-locked door at 68, Place Léon-Blum.

"Madame Pauline Richier? Could we have a word with your son Jean?"

They were both gentle with the pale, well-dressed lady, her blue-rinsed grey hair newly set. Jean had transformed one half of the *salon* into a temporary work-shop, the carpet protected with old newspapers. In his oldest jeans and a paint stained T-shirt he was engrossed in varnishing an eighteenth-century door. On the terrace was its twin, in perfect condition and already refaced with what looked like ancient gilt, except that it was drying in the morning sun.

"Police Judiciaire". Raton and le Bruchec showed their Sûreté Nationale identity cards with the tricolour strip. Jean started to stammer, then sat down in a Louis XVI oval-backed chair. Madame Richier told him to get up; she put a newspaper on the seat cover to protect it from his dirty pants. Jean looked as if he were going to be sick. Raton noted that never had he seen a suspect whose demeanour was more terrified. The Inspector suggested the mother should go in the other room, and

Madame Richier asked them formally if they would take some coffee.

Jean handled the interview which followed with great clumsiness. First he was so overcome with panic that he could hardly stammer out a word. He contradicted himself repeatedly when they asked where he had bought the *fauteuils*. The two inspectors saw at once the way to play this one was gently, until he condemned himself. Thus they set out to reassure Jean; their air was confidential, they nodded understandingly in unison when he explained how in the antiques business one always ran the risk of buying something in good faith, only to discover afterwards that its provenance was questionable.

"It must be a terrible problem for you."

Jean, with great feeling, said it was. Perhaps they were on his side after all. It would be all right, he told himself. No mention so far of château thefts. He remembered that the Judge of Instruction had scared him, especially when he had taken away the chairs from Ménars. But it had been a false alarm.

By the time Madame Richier returned with an immaculate tray laid with bone china coffee cups, her son's stammer had disappeared altogether—he thought he was talking his way out. The visitors sipped their coffee and listened. Jean now felt completely on top. He offered to show them around the apartment.

"I'm not really a restorer—I'm more an expert buyer." The odd voice with the exaggerated "R's" rattled on. "You see these doors here. They aren't very important, but I'm gilding them authentically—you've no idea of the vulgar things they perpetrated with gilt in the last century." The policemen looked interested, and turned their attention to a Louis XVI chair, a twin of the one Madame Richier had been so concerned about, except that its tapestry had been completely stripped. Jean had been pumicing the seat. He showed them the redecoration he had carried out on his beloved mother's bedroom—the draped Louis XVI bed *à baldaquin* (with an overhanging canopy); the new navy-blue wallpaper, heavily embossed with gold *fleur-de-lys*, which Madame Richier pointed out. She hurried into the salon and produced an over-exposed silver framed photograph of her husband in riding gear taken at a polo match in Algiers in the 'thirties. "He was a Colonel in the Chasseurs, you know." The policemen seemed on the point of going, then they hesitated by the door. "Our family has always had a feeling for beautiful things," Pauline told them.

"Yes," said Jean. "We've all inherited the same kind of sensibility. My brother's an artist, too."

"He's also a decorator, perhaps?" asked Raton.

"No—he's a doctor." (From Madame.)

"Here in Paris?"

"No," said Madame. "Xavier lives at Liévin in the Pas-de-Calais."

"You say he's also artistic—what does he do—paint?"

"Not Xavier." Jean cut in. "I was always the one with the gift for draughtsmanship. He collects antiques—all the family's best stuff is there."

Le Bruchec produced his note book for the first time. "Give me his address, please."

Jean's confidence ebbed. He stammered how busy Xavier always was, and that now he thought of it, there wasn't any very interesting furniture there at the moment.

"We'll take his address for the record."

The telephone number came first and then, reluctantly "six bis, rue Thiers". The police made their notes.

"It's no use trying to get him at the moment," Jean told them.

"No," said Madame Richier, "he's away on one of his holidays. He likes to go to North Africa; he was brought up there."

Le Bruchec bowed to her politely, grinning like a wolf.

*   *   *

The Commissaire was lighting a Gitane. Already the office looked as though there had been a small fire. Chevalier had been occupied underlining sections of reports in red ink.

"Well?" The *patron* listened to their account of the interview. When they had finished he sighed: "What's the doctor's address, again?"

He picked up the phone, flicking the sheaf of papers he had been fiddling with across to them at the same time. "Chevalier here. This is urgent. I want a search warrant at once. Yes, it's Dr. Xavier Richier, six bis, rue Thiers, Liévin, Pas-de-Calais. No delays, and arrange with the Lille police to have an inspector there at nine tomorrow morning. And I want you to lay on a photographer, with colour film."

Raton and le Bruchec exchanged a look and examined the papers. The first two were sections of local police reports on the Arras Museum theft in May, 1964, and the Sunday afternoon raid on June 23rd from the St. Pierre Cathedral at Aire, the Boeseghem Chapel, and the Church of Thiennes. In the Arras report Chevalier's underlinings went: *"The supposed thief was balding, below medium height, and wearing glasses. His manner was nervous . . . He wore a well-cut and expensive black suit and silk shirt . . . and was carrying what witnesses described as 'a groundsheet', a 'brown tweed overcoat crumpled up', or 'an old macintosh' . . ."*

In the second report from the Hazebroucke Police the underlinings were: *"*DESCRIPTION*—According to the child, Daniel Vidal, the man seen emerging from the church with the parcel was of medium height and fat. He was sweating and wore either a dirty brown or grey raincoat. . . . Several witnesses identified his car (no number available) as a yellow or beige Renault Dauphine, 1960 or '61 model, in poor condition."*

The final sheet was the Lille police report on Xavier Richier, which had arrived while they were at the Place Léon-Blum.

"Xavier Richier, Doctor, diplomé de Paris, age 44, DESCRIPTION: *5 feet 5 inches tall, inclined to overweight . . . short-sighted and wears glasses . . . has a peculiar twitch and a loud voice . . . dresses very shabbily, often with fly buttons undone . . . laughs and cries very easily . . . drives a Renault Dauphine, registered in Arras on . . ."* there followed the registration number.

CHAPTER XX

The Miniature Museum

As early spring days go in Liévin, Wednesday, March 29th was exceptionally fine. It was cold, but the sun was shining thinly on the slag-heaps and rows of miners' cottages in the valley below Xavier Richier's ill-kempt garden. More pale sunlight reflected from the white walls and rather grubby windows of Richier's villa. For lovers of Liévin, it was a very fine view, but the doctor himself was not there, and in any case his ties with the place had worn thin. "My days here are numbered," he kept insisting to Solange Pridatek, whose deafness had made her no more sensitive to the truth. Three weeks earlier he had taken off on one of the increasingly frequent holiday trips to North Africa.

On this particular morning of the 29th, Dr. Westeel got up as usual at seven-thirty, breakfasted, took a stroll round the garden —he remembers thinking that summer was, at long last, on its way—and then drove to the *Societé de Secours* dispensary in Liévin, where he was responsible for Xavier's morning surgery while the doctor was absent. During his spells filling in at Liévin, Westeel lived in a room on the house's first floor—the only one that was not occupied by Xavier Richier and which, therefore, was not locked and double-locked. Westeel had set off in good time for the surgery. There were twenty or so patients waiting in the hygienic but unaesthetic little room. He put out his cigarette (Westeel hand-rolls them so as not to smoke too many) and settled down calmly to work. His nurse handed him the first filing card.

At ten o'clock the nurse interrupted him apologetically. "There is an urgent phone call for you," she said. "From Solange."

Westeel and Solange, who was very much Xavier's personal housekeeper, did not get on well; the doctor was irritated at being disturbed. Nor could he imagine what urgent matter she could be on about. "I can't speak to her now—tell her we'll call back when we've finished with the patients."

Fifteen minutes later the nurse disturbed him again. "Someone wants to see you urgently. He says he's a policeman."

He was—a member of the Sûreté Nationale from Lille. He asked Westeel to come up to the house straight away as there was something very delicate to be done.

Six bis rue Thiers, when they arrived, was the scene of quite abnormal activity. On the pebble-dash drive, there was a black police Renault 403; smoking a cigarette in the porchway was Joseph le Bruchec, a large impatient figure who was doing his best to ignore the flood of eloquence which Solange was producing in her heavily accented French. She fell on Dr. Westeel, scenting an ally.

"Tell them they're not allowed here. Dr. Richier is not available for appointments of any kind this morning—he'll be away on holiday for another week at least. I'm right, aren't I?"

Le Bruchec, who by this time was thinking that his punctiliousness in waiting to go ahead until Dr. Westeel was present as a witness had been poorly rewarded, clearly felt they were overdoing the kid gloves approach. He showed his *mandat de perquisition* (the French equivalent of a search warrant) to Solange, and barged in—followed by the Lille Inspector and one photographer, equipped with a pair of flash cameras. They had a quick look through the small ground floor area, which contained nothing of interest; and then went upstairs. By now, Solange had stopped her querulous protests and was simply muttering to herself. Even she could see that the burly le Bruchec was not an impressionable kind of person.

Westeel gave him the two keys to the one upstairs room, apart from his own, to which he had access. The police forced the other two, with difficulty because of the double locks. In his three private rooms, Xavier Richier had packed approximately £750,000 worth of furniture, pictures and church furnishings: in such a tiny area, the profusion of chairs and tapestries, faïence and statues, *bibelots* and commodes, was overwhelming. He was in the habit of changing the décor of his rooms incessantly, and the faithful Solange had only been allowed to clean under protest. The largest room of the three was no more than twenty feet by fourteen; the result was like a warehouse of the Louvre. "My God," said the man from Lille, "this isn't a surgery—it's a miniature museum."

They were impressed by the quantity of the material, but as to the quality, they were in doubt. It could conceivably have been the fruit of twenty years' dedicated collecting: the exquisite *fauteuil* in the corner just might, for example, have been an excellent nineteenth-century imitation of one of Boulard's masterpieces. Despite a good deal of practice the police from the G.R.B. were still some way from being in the class of those antique experts who can assess a really valuable piece with one glance. (Even in the upper reaches of the trade the number of connoisseurs who have an instinctive feel for whether an object in their area of speciality is "right" or not, can be counted on the fingers of one hand.)

It seemed possible that the G.R.B. had at last got their hands on the treasure house of the château thieves, but le Bruchec was still not completely sure. His confidence grew when he opened the door of Xavier's bedroom.

A keen amateur collector might reasonably own a fair library of art books; Xavier's, however, was obviously something different. The reference books, in piles from floor to ceiling, covered every conceivable aspect of eighteenth-century furniture and mediaeval ecclesiastical art. Xavier had also filed copies of the two main French country house magazines, *Connaissance des Arts*, and *Maison et Jardin*. Many articles on individual houses, particularly those in the Pas-de-Calais and the Seine-et-Oise, had been minutely annotated in the sprawling blue handwriting that the police were later able to prove without any difficulty was Xavier's—though reading it presented greater problems.

Most interestingly of all, le Bruchec found an old leather-

covered account book, not unlike those game records going back
for years, found in many of the great houses the gang had visited.
Only instead of lists of pheasants and partridges killed on a particular day, the items listed were *fauteuils, écritoires, bonheurs
du jour, guéridons*—indeed virtually every *haute époque* object
from the eighteenth-century masters. There were dates next to
each item, and prices, in some cases very high prices. Another
important piece of evidence was ferreted out during a second
search. It consisted of carbon copies of numerous receipts, and
records of large sums sent to Jean—or received from him. But
for the moment le Bruchec was happy enough with the account
book. Westeel watched him leaning over it, turning the pages,
whistling quietly to himself, and repeating, "My God, two million, would you credit it?" It looked as though they had come
across the gang's inventory (it turned out to be incomplete) of
the treasures that had passed through their hands in a period
of nearly four years. Unfortunately, Richier's personal game-
book omitted the names of the purchasers who had been happy
to get rare and exquisite things at knock-down prices—and look
the other way. But even now, le Bruchec was not one hundred
per cent certain that they had got what they wanted; the genteel
bungalow, the housekeeper, all the trappings of a professional
doctor—exactly the kind of thing he had been brought up to
respect—still made it hard for him to make the final imaginative leap.

He ordered the photographer to get good pictures, including
colour slides, of every article in the locked rooms. They spent
a long morning carrying furniture downstairs and into the garden where the light was better. The villa was chaos, the police
clumping about, and flash bulbs exploding. At one point, they
spread a pinkish tapestry on Xavier's rather bald lawn for the
photographer. It depicted a young woman in a long, flowing
robe talking to an older woman wearing a snood. There was a
group of what looked like bearded Holy Men in the background.
Le Bruchec thought it seemed vaguely familiar, but could not
place where he had seen it before. At least it looked old, he
reckoned, several hundred years at least, judging by the clothes.

The police then interviewed Edouard Westeel, by now a
puzzled and worried man. They were interested in the dates of

the doctor's trips, to North Africa, Paris, and elsewhere, and made a careful note of his scheduled return date—the following Monday, April 3rd. They then descended on the neighbours, who had already enjoyed the most exciting morning in Liévin memory. Le Bruchec got from them a series of more or less reliable anecdotes, including the one about a big man—le Bruchec was convinced it must have been Bihn—relieving himself in the garden. The woman opposite was disappointed to learn that the police were not considering arresting the doctor for this unneighbourly act. It soon emerged that Xavier Richier would not have come top in a Liévin popularity poll.

Their photographs completed, the police punctiliously returned Xavier's collection to its home on the first floor (the doors were no longer locked), said polite goodbyes to Dr. Westeel, who was still confused about what had happened, and less polite ones to Solange, whose frustration had now developed into outrage. Finally they left; the local men to return to Lille, while le Bruchec headed back for the Faubourg St. Honoré as fast as he could. During the four-hour drive back, he became more and more uncertain whether they had finally solved the case, or just succeeded in infuriating a perfectly respectable country doctor. He soon found out. When he heard what had happened, Chevalier ordered a film session in the G.R.B.'s projection room. He began to examine the slides and suddenly jumped in the air: "We've got it, here it is." Le Bruchec, Louis Raton and the rest of the team jostled each other to get a closer look. "We're there," said Chevalier, "there's no mistaking our old friend Esther. I must have studied that picture a hundred times—it's the tapestry from Laval. Bring the dossier with the photos of stolen objects."

It took them two hours to work through all the slides—many of Xavier's items, particularly his enormous collection of church candlesticks, silver cups and statues were totally unidentifiable —they could have come from any one of several hundred French churches. But they did recognise many things they had been hunting so long that Chevalier had often wondered whether they would ever be seen in France again. The big moment came when they showed on the screen a dossier picture of the *grand salon* at the Château de la Cerisaie (as it had been before the château thieves removed a dozen of the most precious items).

"Look at that," called Inspector le Bruchec, "you see the marriage chest on the *secrétaire*, with the coat of arms on the side. Isn't that the same one that we saw in the big room in Liévin—the one next to his bedroom?"

They checked again with the photographs they had taken that morning and, sure enough, there it was—one of the most fascinating museum pieces in France—the marriage chest of Diane of Poitiers. And so the film show continued late into the night, punctuated from time to time by excited shouts from the amateur antique experts.

"Hold it, that's familiar. Yes, I knew it, that's the pair of, what are they called, *cache-pots* in faïence, here it is, faïence de Gilot. They were stolen from the Château de Dampierre."

"So was this *bonheur de jour*—we've got the Duc de Luynes' photos of it here."

"Look at that *fauteuil*. It's one of Geneviève Fath's from Corbeville . . ."

Before the show was over, Chevalier got to his feet. He gave orders for the arrest of Jean Richier, and also of Xavier when he returned to France.

CHAPTER XXI

A True Aristocrat

They lost height before Bordeaux. Caravelle *Normandie*, number FBHRS on Air France Flight 2012 from Casablanca to Paris, suddenly lurched. Xavier Richier, travelling first class, started on the Port Salut (he had already worked his way through smoked salmon, veal steak and fruit salad), and sipped well chilled Pol Roger. It had been a memorable trip, well worth staying the extra weekend, and taking off on impulse for a weekend in Marrakesh. The only disadvantage was that it was now Monday, April 3rd; he should have started work at Liévin that morning.

He presumed Westeel, faithful old Edouard, would have got his cable, though his unplanned itinerary had made any reply out of the question. And also his mother: he wondered whether to stay overnight at Place Léon-Blum, and decided against. Madame Westeel would probably be annoyed enough at his arriving one day late. In his expensive leather suitcase, he had a silver bangle for her from Marrakesh, the vulgarest object he had been able to find, so he presumed she would like it. His present would make everything all right. (As usual, when judging others, he was wrong. Madame Westeel was bitterly angry at the way Xavier took advantage of her young and easy-going husband.)

Xavier peeked out of the window to see if he could get a look at Bordeaux—there was Victor Louis' Grand Theatre, he re-

170

membered, and of course the Cathédral, Saint André. Might be worth a call some time. And there was a fine château just out-side, what was its name? He couldn't for the moment remember, perhaps it would come later. Caravelle *Normandie* circled. All he could see were the neurotically regular pine forests that line the coast route from Bayonne, nothing interesting, only Les Landes, Mauriac country, where Thérèse Desqueyroux, the poisoner, had lived. In its own way this countryside was as sinis-ter as Liévin.

The passengers trouped across the run-way into Bordeaux's unimpressive transit section. Delays, delays, some North African immigrants had lost their vaccination certificates. "Dr. Richier," from the official, studying the passenger list. He glanced at the name on the well-used passport and handed it back without comment. If Xavier had been quicker, perhaps, if it hadn't been for the extra glass of champagne, it might have occurred to him that he hadn't used his medical title when booking the flight a week earlier. Somehow the official must have been expecting him. Instead of wondering, Xavier looked at the luggage piled recklessly high on the trolley, racing across the runway. Pre-sumably it belonged to passengers ending the trip at Bordeaux. Thank God there was no sight of his own valuable suitcases; these idiots were quite capable of taking them off here in error. La Brède, that was it, Château de la Brède—he had visited it years ago with Jean, though only sight-seeing, unfortunately. Lots of good chairs, he recalled. When would Claude be out? He worked it out. He had been given twelve months, like André —the trial had been sometime in November. André had been released on the last day of January, Claude's *liberté provisoire* meant the sentence would run longer, say roughly until the end of the summer.

The passengers waited a long time for the formalities to be completed—largely because Xavier's bags had been unloaded and examined, but not in error. The Bordeaux Police had been warned about their visitor by the G.R.B. Eventually, they re-embarked, strolling across the run-way in the reassuring south-ern sun. Xavier ordered *"du champagne"* in his funny, off-key voice; Air France was doing him proud. But there were sure to be more annoying delays at Paris, he reflected. He was always infuriated by the grotesque system of going to the ground floor to collect luggage, the endless corridors, the canned Wagner.

*　　*　　*

Not this trip. The three men were at the foot of the run-way. "Dr. Xavier Richier," a flash of *Police Judiciaire* cards, and still squeaking a stream of terrified protest, he was in the back of a police Renault 403 screaming its priority officiously all the way through the airport and on to the outside lane of the Fontaine-bleau-Paris Autoroute. Lights flashing, they exceeded the speed limit by 50 k.p.h. (30 m.p.h.) all the way in. They were at the Place d'Italie a mere twenty minutes after the Caravelle had grounded; normally, Xavier would have been lucky even to have passed through the customs in that time. But all this dispatch was simply part of the V.I.P. treatment which Le Patron had carefully arranged for the doctor's reception.

The top men had turned out in his honour; le Bruchec and Louis Raton examined the jumpy, plump Richier with unconcealed curiosity, and something approaching chagrin. Could this, they wondered, be the great criminal, the *Gentleman Cambrioleur* architect of the Le Mans theft, Laval, Dampierre, and . . . what a list. The odd way he had of poking his little nose up in the air, as if he wanted to be taller. He looked so timid. It seemed a let-down. They were irritated with him for failing to live up to their idea of what he should be—as irritated as they had been after St. Denis. Had they got the wrong man after all? Surely it was impossible.

Soon all doubts were resolved.

As befitted the other leading actor in the final act Chevalier was awaiting the climax off-stage—in his office. When they brought the doctor in—by now his escort had grown to nearly a dozen—Xavier blinked around the room. His face, twitching with fright, was framed against the long line of well-thumbed files, most of them referring to him, indirectly at least. They all might have been an exhaustive research dossier for his bizarre biography.

"Come with us to the Projection Room, please, Doctor Richier. My name's Chevalier, Commissaire Chevalier. I'm going to show you a film."

Le Patron opened the confrontation as urbanely as a diplomat.

A whole series of exhibits flashed on the screen in turn: the Laval tapestry, its dense purples and greens still glowing after nearly half a millennium; the Arras *jardinière*; a pair of exquisite Boulard *fauteuils* from Corbeville, marvels of grace and strength; Notre Dame de Joyel, which Xavier had so meticulously cleaned and restored. (When the curé at Thiennes later had the statue returned to his church, he had difficulty in recognising it. He despatched it to his superior, the Bishop at Arras, to find out whether or not it had been defaced. His Grace consulted an expert and then advised the curé there was no need to worry. "I am told Notre Dame has been restored with exquisite care, and that now one can truly appreciate the work of the master who carved her so long ago.")

Finally the camera focused on the marquetry top of one of the *bonheurs du jour* from the Duc de Luynes at Dampierre. The film stopped.

"A wonderful piece," said Chevalier.

"Yes," said Xavier cautiously.

"How much do they pay you at Liévin, 4,000 francs (roughly £300) a month, isn't it?"

Xavier confirmed this with a rapid nod.

"Now then," said Chevalier deprecatingly. "You're an expert on these matters. I'm just a layman, a philistine even, I suppose. Tell me, out of interest—supposing I was lucky enough to own a table like that, and I needed to turn it into cash. I probably would, too. How much would I get for it?"

In a mere five minutes in the murky offices they had already reached the turning point in one of the simplest interrogations Chevalier had ever conducted, an anti-climax at the end of his most difficult case. Xavier hesitated, but he could not resist answering. A professional criminal would have stood pat, asked for a lawyer, and pleaded total ignorance. As Raton and le Bruchec had realised at the Place Léon-Blum, the way to interrogate the Richier family was to bait them with the chance to boast. Xavier began his reply awkwardly, inhibited by fear. By the end he was in his best lecturing form, the style he so enjoyed, and which had finally broken Mabilotte's nerves and patience. Now it broke Xavier himself.

"Well, that would depend," he began. "If you were to try in August, say—of course, that's the worst month of the year . . ."

"The worst?"

"Oh yes, a terrible month for sales. Well, then you might be lucky to get £5,500. On the other hand, in November or December, on a good day in Drouot, you might get as much as £9,000. But that would be the very top price," the doctor pontificated: "I would advise a reserve of, say, £7,500—that would be a fair figure." The doctor looked round unhappily for a moment, like a child who had said something he had expected adults would find funny, but had inexplicably gone down the wrong way. Chevalier cut in quickly to reassure him, and motioned the other police to stay silent.

"Fascinating. So just a few months can make all that difference."

"Oh yes, for instance, on one occasion I remember . . ." the corn-crake voice rasped on for several minutes, while Chevalier smiled encouragingly. Xavier was beginning to look happier. At forty-four, he had still not learnt how feeble he was as an advocate; he had never acquired the ability to gauge his impact on others. Now he was even beginning to conquer his fear; perhaps he would be able to win this friendly-looking policeman over; perhaps, even, it was all a mistake. He went on for a good five minutes, Chevalier nodding as if deeply satisfied at learning the answer to a question about which he had always been deeply curious.

"To get back to that particular table we saw on the screen a few minutes ago," said Le Patron silkily. "You must have paid a good price for it."

Xavier hesitated again. "I saved nearly two years' salary to buy that."

"Even that's cheap, isn't it?"

"Oh yes," said Xavier, "of course if you know where to go, and can pick out something good no one else has paid any attention to, it often happens . . ." He went on again in his lecturing manner, and ended: "That's what being an expert means."

"I see," said Chevalier. "I suppose you've got a bill for that table you'd be able to find?"

Xavier looked evasive and finally said yes.

"Good. Now let's see some more items from your remarkable collection," Chevalier continued. They dimmed the lights and this time showed a series of ecclesiastical objects, mainly statuettes, but also candelabra, silver altar-ware of various kinds, a silver holy-water ewer, statues in wood and stone—a small cross-section of his "religious" room, where Westeel's daughter, Caroline, now has her bed, under wallpaper decorated with teddy bears. (The police had no idea where any of them had come from: some have not been identified even now.)

"A remarkable collection," said Chevalier, "where did you get them all? Those mediaeval statues, for example, they must have cost a fortune."

"Oh no," said Xavier, for once truthfully. "Far from it. It's really amazing what you can pick up in old churches."

Le Patron smiled tersely.

"Is it now?"

Xavier was almost sure he was beaten. When he started to talk again it was more to comfort himself than in the hope of convincing anyone.

"If you offer a priest some money to help his restoration fund, or offer to do some work yourself, have central heating installed, that kind of thing, well, they're often delighted to let you take a lot of things away in exchange. They have no idea of the value of things, they're very ignorant. They often assume that because something is ancient it must be without value—that's how people think in Liévin. Everything's got to be the latest—no respect at all for the past."

Chevalier thought for the first time that the doctor might be telling at least part of the truth. The Commissaire knew that only that month the Bishop of Paris had sent a diocesan message to every parish priest in the country about preserving the Church's property from unscrupulous decorators who for some time had been working as Xavier had described, often with disastrous results. Recently, they had been able to take advantage of the Vatican Council decisions on relics and church furniture. These had encouraged many enthusiastic, ecumenically minded young priests to try and turn their churches into the nearest they could get to a Quaker meeting house, so determined were they to purge doubtful items. Often rare and precious objects had been consigned to attics. Decorators were making a profession of kind offers to clear away the old junk for nothing. Others toured remote areas offering to "modernise" churches at cut prices, and in the process picking up irreplaceable objects for nothing.

"The Church often looks after its possessions badly," said Chevalier.

"The Beaux Arts are worse," Xavier replied. And launched an attack on the incompetence and philistinism of this worthy organisation, plus a series of stories demonstrating his point, including one of his favourite gripes—the eighteenth-century chairs at Arras, which had been repainted *"au repolin"* and been completely ruined.

"I see you like faïence," said Chevalier. The Duc de Luynes' amphorae appeared on the screen.

"How much did you pay for that pair of, what are they, Greek vases?"

"Eighteenth-century models of the Roman."

"Oh yes," said Le Patron, "Now, tell me what you gave for those."

"I can't remember," said Xavier.

"I didn't think you would. How long have you had them?"

"Oh, three years, I suppose."

"You couldn't have had them that long. They were stolen less than two years ago."

"Stolen?"

"Yes, it was in May 1963 when you robbed the Duc de Luynes' château at Dampierre. These *fauteuils*, of course, came from Ménars, as you probably remember. And these chests, this extraordinary one with the coat of arms of Diane of Poitiers on it, for instance, I expect you remember taking that from the Château de la Cerisaie."

"I didn't take it."

"No?" said Le Patron. "What about this then?" and he showed the double arrow mark *jardinière* from the Saint Vaast Museum at Arras.

To everyone's surprise—half a dozen members of the G.R.B.,

plus the stenographer, had been listening in silence since the beginning—Xavier started to laugh. "Yes, I took that. I'm surprised they even missed it when you think how the Beaux Arts people treat their things. It was in broad daylight, too."

"Hadn't you been talking to one of the officials about faïence a bit earlier on?"

"Yes—he reckoned he was an expert, but of course he knew nothing, like the fool who had the chairs repainted. I would never have done a thing like that with *my* chairs—they're all in better condition now than when I got them."

"Then you took them to improve them?"

"Of course, why else? You should have seen some of those statues when I got them, a disgrace to the Church. You remember that bust, it's actually a statuette of Saint Innocent, which I took from the Musée de la Chartreuse at Douai . . ."

Once Xavier had started, there was no stopping him. On and on he went, thoroughly enjoying himself, while the police listened in amazement to the croaking febrile voice. The stenographer was nearing the end of her notebook.

"Why did you start to steal?" asked Chevalier. "To make money?"

"Never," said Xavier. "Never, never." Tears of emotion appeared in the fishy eyes and rolled down his cheeks from behind the heavy glasses. It was a mixture of convoluted rationale, confession and the kind of diatribe against petty officialdom that might have come from an Opposition Deputy making a set speech. "Everywhere I saw artistic treasures ruined, neglected, ignored and defaced, even in the most important museums. In a sentence, I stole in order to care for things and restore objects which were left to rot through the carelessness and indifference (he used the word *carence*) of the Beaux Arts. My sensibility . . ."

Never in a life-time could Xavier have said anything about himself in one sentence. The words flooded out, trying to communicate his personal, crazy logic. Chevalier smoked and listened. After so long, he understood—of course, this neurotic doctor was only telling part of the truth, the part that showed him in the best light, and there was no doubt he had stolen for profit. (Later, much later, the police were able to calculate that almost precisely seventy per cent of all the items stolen were resold.) And yet, what he was saying made a kind of sense, and explained so many things Chevalier had puzzled about. In a way he had been right, the man was a kind of *Gentleman Cambrioleur*, but odder, and more obsessive than he had ever guessed. Xavier's voice croaked on, the tears now finished and the eyes shining hotly behind the glasses.

Not that Chevalier learnt the full story even then—by a long way. None of the G.R.B. realised how close they had come to losing their precious evidence at the eleventh hour. The doctor's collection, the variegated proof of his larceny—and also his attempt to create the grand, aristocratic style of an eighteenth-century château in his *bijou* villa—had nearly disappeared.

On Thursday, March 30th the telephone had rung at the doctor's villa. Solange Pridatek answered. Madame Pauline Richier, whom Solange worshipped, shouted a series of instructions at the half-deaf old maid. Pauline Richier had been told by Jean what to say, without understanding its significance. Even now she adheres to a theory only a loving mother could believe—that her boys were innocents, framed by the unscrupulous Mabilotte.

"Solange," she screeched. "You have got to move all Dr. Xavier's old furniture and statues and things. Start immediately transferring everything to your own apartment. We'll be sending a van from Paris as soon as possible."

Solange, who to this day does not understand what all the fuss was about (she believes that "Dr. Xavier" only had a lot of old bric-à-brac that priests like Curé Bernaud had given him to play with) started to do what she was told. But Edouard Westeel arrived an hour later. He promptly forbade Solange to move anything. He even took the keys off her.

Westeel was a worried man. He had understood from the police something of the size of the affair, and was guiltily remembering all the heavy cases he had transported in his kindly way for Xavier. He was worried that someone might try to remove the evidence. He had never liked the look of that big thug, Marcel, the one they had called "Karim". Supposing he showed up?

He needn't have worried. Jean was arrested by the police the

following day, protesting his innocence to the last. And as for
Marcel Bihn, he disappeared from his shop on the Quai Malaquais altogether. The police only managed to arrest him ten
months later—on February 6th, 1966. By this time, both Huré
and Mabilotte had long since joined the Richier brothers in
the Prison of Fresnes. And the police were still making investigations, trying to establish where the stolen items had come from
and, an even more difficult job, where the enormous number
that had disappeared altogether had been sold.

Finally, Xavier stopped talking. They took him away. The
G.R.B. team had a rapid celebratory drink, and Chevalier prepared a Press statement for release that night—the first assessment of the value of the gang's total haul over the years was
over thirty million new francs (£3 million). It comfortably out-
distanced the British Train Robbers.

But the affair was still not completed. For over three years
three judges of instruction and a leading judge, Maître Aveur-
seing at Pontoise, worked to unravel the distribution system, to
assess guilt, and trace the proceeds of over seventy different raids.
Only in 1968 were the five members of the syndicate finally
brought to trial and convicted.

They were charged with seventy-six specific "operations",
though the prosecution claimed there were many more they had
failed to prove. In any case seventy-six was quite enough and
the examining magistrate's dossier, a mound of lime green files,
ran to over a million words. President Perrot, the judge in
charge, looked vaguely Pickwickian with his red robes and bald
pate. He seemed shocked that the thieves had been able to
function with such contemptuous ease.

In the dock Claude Mabilotte thought this might work as
a mitigating factor and tried his hand at an extempore defence.
Owners who were so casual with their property, he implied en-
gagingly, had only themselves to blame if it were stolen. "Anyway I never understood why people were crazy enough to pay
a fortune for a few sticks of old wood." It was the familiar voice
of Claude the hard-headed businessman, though now anyone
could see he was bankrupt. André Huré, as evasive as ever,
backed up his old partner, but without much conviction. He

looked beaten but over three years in jail awaiting trial had left him as boyish as before. This was lucky for him because immaturity was virtually the only defence he had to offer. Marcel Bihn now looked thinner—the well-pressed suit smelled of moth-balls, he had lost his old physical authority in Pontoise Prison. Jean Richier, also lighter and slighter, sat next to Xavier who wore a flowing necktie of heavy silk recalling grander days. They kept pretty quiet and throughout the proceedings Jean's hand grasped Xavier's, offering fraternal comfort.

The prisoners' evident wretchedness was a help; it made them look smaller than lifesize. Surely Xavier, his watery eyes flickering with distaste over a truly deplorable plaster statue of Justice above the president, surely this eccentric little man could not be a criminal genius? One of the team of prosecution lawyers said as much. In a blanket accusation, which seemed to be levelled against the Paris antiques trade as a whole, he speculated that "Mr. Big", the real brains behind the syndicate, might still be at large. No one paid much attention to this except Xavier himself, nettled by the implied belittlement. As soon as there was a chance he made one of his old speeches presenting himself as a kind of aesthetic Peter Pan, collecting and guarding neglected treasures. "So many objects were in such a bad state that I could not permit myself to leave them in jeopardy—*morally*."

Jean offered an encouraging hand squeeze but the rest of the gang did not try to hide their irritation. The doctor's moral fervour had always been a bore. But by the end of each session he was entirely deflated. Each time President Perrot ordered a recess police wearing the white *kepi*, symbol of authority, snapped on the handcuffs and led the dejected gang off, a process watched with interest by the local housewives in the public gallery. These kibitzers were accustomed to a stronger diet of titillating detail but were fascinated by the weird recital of polychrome virgins and gueridons, even if there was no sex or violence involved. From long experience they deduced that here was one case which had no chance of ending in a triumphal acquittal and celebration champagne in the Café du Sport down the road. The view in the Pontoise public gallery was that the prosecutor was going to get the ten-year sentences he was asking for.

But the local ladies had read it wrong. The court spent three hours and twenty minutes reaching its collective decision, and the sentences were milder than some defence lawyers had feared. Bihn, seven years; Mabilotte, six; Huré and Jean Richier, five each; and then—a faint whoosh of surprise around the disinfected courtroom—five for Xavier too, but the sentence to be suspended. This meant that as long as he avoided any more trouble he would be a free man.

Cristobel Gonzalez-Sotto, the craftsman from rue de Charonne, who had done so much work for the syndicate, had brought a light touch to the proceedings. He was particularly keen to emphasize his heterosexuality—at one stage he produced a wife to back him up. He had vociferously insisted that the retouching and recarving he had done for Marcel Bihn was no different from the kind of work he specialised in for dozens of Paris antique dealers. Gonzalez-Sotto said he had no reason to believe any of the furniture brought to him had been stolen, and the court believed him. When the verdict was announced, he beamed triumphantly, and black moustache bristling, left Pontoise with his wife on his arm.

All round it seemed pretty fair. The court had avoided undue harshness and at the same time they had shown an appropriate concern for the defence of property. Xavier was scarcely the disinterested saviour of threatened beauty he liked to make out, but insofar as so abstract a quality can be assessed, he seemed the least criminal of the gang. And he had been in prison off and on for over three years while the investigation was prepared. The other four would go back, Bihn to the prison library which he was recataloguing, Jean Richier to continue his work on the frescoes in the chapel which, in much the same spirit as Alain Michel in Poitiers, he had volunteered to refurbish.

But the conclusion was not entirely satisfactory either for the châteaux owners or the police. Only a fraction of the stolen property had been recovered and in restitution the syndicate were only being required to pay the sum of just under £40,000 (451,000 Francs). Even though the original police estimates of the total value of the thefts may have been exaggerated (it was enormously weighted by the largely hypothetical prices of such objects as the tapestries from Le Mans and Laval) the owners were understandably furious. But as all the gang claimed to be broke there was little the court could do. The French State itself came off worst. It was awarded token damages of one franc (one shilling and eightpence or, say, a quarter).

And then there was the question of the antiques and other objects which somehow had left France for London and New York. Those involved with the investigations remain convinced that the route was through Belgium or Holland, probably both. But, despite forty months of investigation, they were still unable to name the guilty men, or even discover the identities of unscrupulous London or New York clients who were happy to buy rare objects without worrying too much about their source. The gang had shown themselves ready enough to incriminate one another but on this part of the operation refused flatly to say anything. So in a sense the trial was a failure.

The story had ended, in effect, at the moment when Xavier started his diatribe against the Beaux Arts. The rest was just the laborious mopping up process necessary to conclude one of the most complex criminal enterprises of modern times.

The long-suffering Jacques Dupont had the last word. (He has still found no trace of his precious chairs from Bussy-le-Grand or, even more frustrating and mysterious, the great silver altar-piece from St. Denis.) The night of the arrest, he had appeared on television to congratulate the police, and tell the French public how important it was for their country's cultural heritage that the gang had finally been arrested.

"Richier was no ordinary thief," Dupont said, which was truthful, but commendably generous in the circumstances, perhaps even over-generous. "This man was a genuine scholar. And as for understanding *objets d'art*—he was a true aristocrat."